# GET A GRIP!

*What to Do at the End of Your Rope*

By Zona Hayes-Morrow

Harrison House
Tulsa, OK

*Get A Grip!*
*What to Do at the End of Your Rope*
ISBN: 987-160683-888-4
Copyright © 2013 Zona Hayes-Morrow
Published by Harrison House Publishers
Tulsa, Oklahoma

# FOREWORD

Zona's book *Get A Grip* is wonderful and will be so helpful to all who read it. Since I have known Zona for over forty years, I can attest to the fact that she has hung onto God's Word and that has kept her alive and the mighty woman of God she is today. Her dad Norvel Hayes would never give up on her, and she has been such a devoted and loving daughter to him.

I salute this remarkable lady for sharing her thoughts to help and strengthen us.

Dodie Osteen
Co-Founder of Lakewood Church

I really believe that you will enjoy this book written by my daughter, Zona. I have watched her face death about 13 times over the years. I heard the doctor tell her one time that she only had 30 days to live but she got a grip on God's Word that promised her victory. Zona had learned that she needed to confess the victory promised in the Word of God and put her trust in Him. And I watched her do just that. She overcame death that time and many other times. If you will only believe and confess victory, then you too can overcome whatever you're facing. The truth of God's Word says that all things are possible to him that believeth but you can't have any doubt. Put your faith in God alone and He will share the victory with you. I suggest that you read this book and get a grip on the truth found in God's Word so that you too can find victory. God says in the Book of Psalms to offer

God thanksgiving for anything He's promised you. And God promises that in the day of your trouble that He will come to you and deliver you then when you receive your miracle, you need to glorify the Lord. I believe with you that by reading this book that you can learn to overcome any attack from the enemy. Learn to obey God and thank Him for victory before you see the final results. When you put your trust in the Lord and rely on Him, you will enjoy your life like God says in the Book of Job then all of your days will be prosperous, full of joy, strength and victory. I pray that God will have mercy upon you and that you will learn to trust Him to bring you victory because He loves you so very, very much.

Dr. Norvel Hayes
Founder, Norvel Hayes Ministries

# CONTENTS

# INTRODUCTION

*Get a Grip!* is a dynamic, life-changing book for every believer who is desperate to know what to do when you come to the end of your rope. Many times in my life I felt that I was at the end of my rope, but I learned how to hang on and "get a grip" by going forward in the midst of great adversity.

In this book I will share parts of my personal testimony, including how I was delivered from eating disorders, drug addiction, numerous health problems and attacks on my life, as well as being healed from personal tragedies. I will show you how I learned to walk in victory.

Today, I am a picture of health because I learned to get a grip. I know that if I hadn't held on to my faith in God's Word, I wouldn't be alive today. If you are going through great adversity and want to know what you need to do to overcome and tighten your grip on life, healing, health, victory, joy, peace, freedom, and prosperity, then this book is for you!

I pray this book will inspire you to move forward through any storm, attack, or adversity that appears to be hopeless.

Learn how to tighten your grip and receive every benefit that belongs to you in Christ. If you had a bad report and you feel like you are at the end of your rope, I want to challenge you with the uncompromised Word of God to never look at the bad report, but rather keep your eyes on Jesus and get a grip on God's report of life and victory.

Enjoy the freedom that comes from going after God with all your strength, heart, and mind; then you will no longer be satisfied with compromise, worry, fear, poverty, depression, failure, defeat, oppression, struggles, wrong relationships and an old mindset.

I refused to settle for the enemy's lies and refused to live a mediocre life. I decided I would go higher up the mountain to get my health and God's best. As you read this book, expect the faith of God to come alive in you. Step into new realms of victory where you have never been before, and you will have God's best for your life!

# 1
# HANG ON TO GOD'S PRESENCE

I have been at the end of my rope and faced death thirteen times. Regardless of whatever you are dealing with or facing in your life, I have been there and I can help you get to the other side of the mountain in your life. I have been through anorexia, bulimia, kidney failure, dialysis, anemic blood condition, low potassium to the point that I was not able to walk, and many other life threatening situations. I learned how to get into the presence of God and hold on to His promises until I reached the mountaintop with victory in every situation.

## Hang on to God's Word and It Will Save Your Life

When I felt I was at the end of my rope, I learned to get a grip on God's Word. Before God changed me, I used to take His Word for granted, but I have since learned to treasure it and His presence.

Many years ago, I didn't realize the value of the testimonies and messages I heard my dad preach. I would think, *Well, here we go again with the same story.* I knew all of my dad's stories and could repeat them verbatim. But even though I listened to what he was saying, I never heard the message that he was trying to share.

I measured his services by the length of his sermon or the story he told, instead of gleaning the truth he was trying to impart. I had the wrong attitude. However, when God changed me, I became excited when my dad shared his testimonies and spoke about what God had done for me.

I've learned to never take God's Word or His blessings for granted. We need to reject wrong thoughts as soon as they come and respect the truth of the Bible in order for God's truth to grow on the inside of us. Our thoughts are seeds in the garden of our hearts. If we respect the anointed messages we hear, they will save our lives.

I didn't realize the messages I heard my dad preach would later save my life. In 1994, all of my symptoms seemed to indicate I was not going to make it. I was getting blood clots inside my mouth. I managed to hide them for a long time from my family and co-workers by wiping them out of my mouth with a Kleenex and burying the Kleenex in the trash can. However, my mouth would instantly begin to fill up with blood again. Finally, a lady who was traveling with me found one of those bloody Kleenex and confronted me.

I was getting ready to go on vacation when God spoke to me and revealed that I needed to see a Spirit-filled doctor named Dr. Fowler. God told me that I had something wrong with my parathyroid and kidneys. We stopped by Dr. Fowler's house on the way to Florida and he While I was in the hospital, the spirit of death came into my room. Dr. Fowler was going to release me, but I didn't want to leave the hospital and was too weak to walk. My dad told the girls who traveled with me that I would die if I stayed in the hospital, so he had them pick me up, carry me out, and bring me to his house.

My dad began yelling that he wasn't going to let me die. He had one of the girls get on one side of me while he got on the other side and together they dragged me up and down the driveway, all the while making me say, "I will live and not die." As I continued to speak the Word of God over my situation, I got stronger and stronger. By about the fiftieth trip, I was running up and down the driveway shouting, "I will live and not die!"

After Dr. Fowler reviewed the test results he said, "Zona, I love you like a daughter and I know you're a woman of faith, but in the natural, you need to get your affairs in order because you've got about thirty days to live."

I went outside and began looking at all of the colors. They seemed so much brighter to me. I told God, "I can't do this. I just want to go ahead and come home now." Then all of a sudden, something hit me in my gut and I heard the word "Fight." As soon as I heard that word, it was like life came into me. I knew I could do this, even though my emotions were going crazy on the inside. I looked at the doctor and boldly declared, "I'm not going to die!"

He said, "Zona, I'm going to believe with you."

The next day I agreed to surgery. They put a fistula in my arm and I began dialysis. I could have allowed myself to give in to that sickness. I could have taken on a "poor me" attitude, and that would have killed me. But instead, I chose to hold on to God's Word and live. If I hadn't fought for my miracle, I could have died. But that wasn't God's will or His best for my life; it was *my* choice.

We have to choose to go for God's best. God doesn't want us to settle for anything less than His perfect will for our lives. He doesn't want us to settle for second best. He doesn't want us to just survive and get by. He desires that we move higher up His mountain.

## Hang on to Speaking Life

By speaking words of life, I climbed my mountain in faith. In order for us to go up God's mountain and have miraculous results, we have to speak life, not death. There is great power in our words when we line them up with God's Word. Words can bring us either life or death (Proverbs 18:21).

I really learned the power of words when I had forty-two growths on my body as a teenager. I was very embarrassed of all of the warts I had; they were all over my body. I begged my dad to take me to the doctor to have them cut off, but they always seemed to come back (and bring more with them). After a few years, my dad decided it didn't do any good to have them cut off, so he stopped taking me to the doctor.

My dad was good friends with Kenneth Hagin, Sr. Once, I was at a friend's house when Brother Hagin was visiting and he asked me how I was doing. I told him I had "dad" problems and proceded to tell him the whole story, While we were talking, my dad walked in. Brother Hagin related what I had been saying and then laughed, saying, "Oh Norvel, that is easy. I can just curse the warts and they'll disappear."

My dad was going to ask about that later, but before he could, the Lord spoke to Brother Hagin and told him to go see his sister because it would be the last time he would see her before God brought her to heaven. So my dad began to seek God for an answer instead. He sought God for several weeks before he finally got the answer he needed.

One day as he was walking through the house, all of a sudden God took him to heaven and asked him, "How long are you going to put up with the growths on your daughter's body?"

My dad said, "What do You mean? I don't have anything to do with them."

My dad knew that he had made God mad because God responded in a loud voice saying, "You're the head of your house! Whatever you let go on in your house is your fault! If you will curse those growths at the root, just like I cursed the fig tree, then they'll die and disappear. But you've got to believe and not doubt, son!"

My dad returned from heaven and came into the living room where I was sitting with my boyfriend. He knelt down in front of me and put his hands on my knees, and made my boyfriend put his hands over my dad's hands. Then he prayed for me and cursed the growths just like Jesus told him to do. I was embarrassed and thought my dad had flipped out, but he was just standing in faith for my miracle.

I had no faith and didn't believe anything that my dad was doing, yet his faith didn't waver. All day every day, he would say, "Thank You, Lord, for removing the growths from my daughter's body." He would say it all the time. Every time he would pray or bless the food, he would thank the Lord for removing the growths from my body. He would sing it to me. Any time he would talk to me, he would say it. I got so frustrated with him!

I counted the growths every day. When Dad would say something about God removing the growths from my body,, I would stick my hands in his face and say, "See they're all still here! Your prayers aren't working and you're driving me crazy!" He would merely shake his head and say, "No, I don't see anything. All I see is clear skin. Thank you, Lord, for removing the growths from my daughter's body."

Three months later, I was counting the growths and noticed there were eight missing. I looked everywhere but couldn't find them, so I went to my dad and said, "I count my warts every day and there are forty-two of them. Today, I counted them and there were only thirty-four. Where did the other eight go?"

My dad got so excited he started dancing around and said, "What do I care where they went? They're gone and the other thirty-four have no choice but to leave as well! Thank you, Lord, for removing the growths from my daughter's body!"

Then three months later, the day came when I was totally free from all the warts on my body. They were all gone! My dad showed me by example how to talk like God talks and have miraculous results. He wouldn't waver from his confession of faith. He refused to speak the problem, and through this he was teaching me how to call those things that be not as though they were (Romans 4:17).

Later in my life, I learned how to apply the knowledge I gained by overcoming these growths and what it meant to speak the Word of God with boldness. After I gave my heart to Jesus, I began to climb God's mountain by confessing His promises, instead of the problem. This became a lifestyle of walking up the mountain by faith and not by sight.

## Hang on to Every Life-Giving Word

Today, I treasure every life-giving word because I learned that these words can make the difference for me in whether I live or die. I heard the Bible and messages of faith before, but they were only messages, not the Word of God bringing me life. I didn't understand that I would need to use those teachings and testimonies my dad shared so I could learn to speak the Word for myself. Now I treasure everything that I've learned from my dad and the Word of God and have learned to speak the Word for myself.

Recently, after a service with my dad, I thought to myself, *I'm hanging on to every word he says. Every word that comes out of his mouth is anointed. Every word is an oracle from God. I don't want to miss one service when he teaches the Word!* When we have this kind of respect for God's Word, I guarantee we will understand what the Word is saying.

Through the years, I traveled with my dad to different places as he ministered, as he repeated the same testimonies over and over again. There comes a time in our lives when we need the messages we have heard and the Word we have read, because the devil hates us and will attack us. When he does, God's Word is the first line of defense that will enable us to overcome.

## Hang on by Seeking God's Presence

When I felt like I was at the end of my rope, I tightened my grip by seeking God's presence. Often when people get to the end of their rope, they start looking to people and things to hold on to. We need to have friends who will help us get our eyes off of our problems and back on God.

I love what Moses did. In the Bible, it says that Moses brought the people to meet God. He didn't just tell them what God was saying, he took them to meet God for themselves. *"And Moses brought the people out of the camp to meet with God, and they stood at the foot of the mountain. Now Mount Sinai was completely in smoke, because the LORD descended upon it in fire. Its smoke ascended like the smoke of a furnace, and the whole mountain quaked greatly. And when the blast of the trumpet sounded long and became louder and louder, Moses spoke, and God answered him by voice"* (Exodus 19:17-19 NKJV).

Can you imagine being in the presence of God when it is that strong? We need the presence of God. Sometimes the presence of God touches people and is so overwhelming they can't move and can hardly breathe. One thing we can be sure of, in His presence, we find everything we need.

# Hang on
# by Going to God

When I felt like I was at the end of my rope, I had to keep going to God and focusing on Him. I had to get my eyes off my circumstances, problems, adversities, sorrows and fears. We can only go higher by abiding in God's presence.

Today, many people are distracted by worldly things, so they stop climbing the mountain and become complacent. I made sure this wouldn't happen to me because I determined that I would never stop my climb. We need to realize that the devil is a liar, and he will use tricks to try to kill, steal, and destroy us. Thank God my dad taught me this. It saved my life. There is nothing good about the devil. His sole purpose is to get us off track so we will never fulfill our destinies.

Moses went up to God; Jesus came down to earth in the form of a man. Jesus gave His life as a ransom for many. He came down to where we are. Jesus loves us so much that He reaches us where we are. He came down to meet us, save us, and fill us with the Holy Spirit.

## Hang on to High Standards
## and go up into a Higher Realm

I refuse to risk my life, peace, joy, health or any of the blessings of God by compromising or lowering my standards. I keep my standards built on God's Word. I refuse to back down for anything.

The spirit of this age is bringing down everything and will try to tear us down as well, if we allow him to do so. I keep my eyes off what people say and keep my focus on Jesus. Moses didn't allow the troubles around him to distract him from going up the mountain. He went up to meet God. I had to do the same thing to get my eyes off my troubles.

Are we determined to go up to a higher level where there is no sickness or poverty, to rise above anything that is keeping us from victory in our lives? I had to change my attitude and mindset to live above the norm and go up to a higher level, to gain victory over the devil's mind games and secure God's best for me. Our thoughts matter—how we view ourselves, who we are, what we are called to do, and where we're called to go. All of these things are influenced by our thoughts.

## Hang on to Pleasing God with a Lifestyle of Obedience

I had to get a grip on pleasing God through a lifestyle of obedience in order to continue to ascend my mountain. Obedience is the key to receiving God's benefits. God has already done the work, but we have to choose to walk in obedience to His Word to get where we need to be.

We choose to obey God's voice. Sometimes, we question whether it is Him speaking to us or not. He may tell us to do something, and we wonder if it is His voice or our flesh. That is why we need to learn to hear and recognize the voice of the Lord and know His heart. Then we will be able to understand what He is saying to us.

In order to live the life that God has prepared for us, we need to follow the path that He has set before us and obey His direction. If we choose to do our own thing, we may miss out on blessings that He has prepared for us or walk into trouble that He was trying to help us avoid.

After nearly dying several times, I realized that my daddy's money couldn't buy my healing. I realized that the people he knew wouldn't make a difference regarding whether or not I received my healing. It is not about the people we know, how much money we have, or who we are related to - we have to go up to meet God for ourselves. We have to choose to walk in His Word.

Going higher in our relationship with the Lord requires that we walk in obedience to Him like Moses did. I'm not talking about only obeying the Lord sometimes, when it works with our schedule or is comfortable. I'm talking about a lifestyle of obedience and studying to show ourselves approved unto God.

We must rightly divide the Word by using our authority to think, talk, and walk like Jesus. We do this by simply applying the Word in every area of our lives. We have to know God's will for our lives and who we are in Christ, as well as the benefits He has given us and how to apply them. That is why we must study God's Word.

## Hang on to Your
## Authority of God's Word

When we feel like we are at the end of our rope, we need to hold on to the authority of God's Word. We must be bold and take authority over the devil. We can't get soft with the devil. We can't compromise. We must refuse to let him steal our health, joy, peace, finances, and loved ones.

To walk in healing, we must take authority over the symptoms in our bodies and tell the devil to get away from us. We take authority over the symptoms by speaking the Word to them. Daily, I curse symptoms at the root and refuse to agree with them. Symptoms don't mean that we are sick. However, when we agree with even the slightest symptom, we allow the devil to bring more sickness. When we take authority over the symptoms, we are disagreeing with them and not allowing them to take root in our bodies. This is how we stop the devil's plan to kill, steal, and destroy our health.

We have to know our place in Christ. We are seated with Christ in heavenly places, which means that we are far above anything this world or the devil has to offer. The Bible says, *"But God, who is rich in mercy, because of His great love with which He loved us, even when we were dead in trespasses, made us alive together with Christ (by grace you have been saved), and raised us up together, and made us sit together in the heavenly places in Christ Jesus"* (Ephesians 2:4-6 NKJV).

We need to continue to stay focused on where we are seated. The devil is under our feet. We have to walk in our God-given authority and live above the attacks of the enemy.

## Hang on by Walking with the Mindset of Jesus

I choose to live by the standards of Jesus Christ because I am far above the world's standards. God's Word says, *"Do not be conformed to this world, but be transformed by the renewing of your mind, that you may prove what is that good and acceptable and perfect will of God"* (Romans 12:2 NKJV).

Even when it comes to physical sickness, people say, "Well, everybody is getting it." The world sees themselves in the storm, but God's Word says, *"No evil will conquer you; no plague will come near your home"* (Psalm 91:10 NLT).

Many say, "Well, everybody is getting the flu." It should be no surprise then, when they begin to see themselves getting the flu. God's Word says that we are seated above the flu. The world says, "Everybody is struggling financially," but God's Word says, *"This Book of the Law shall not depart from your mouth, but you shall meditate in it day and night, that you may observe to do according to all that is written in it. For then you will make your way prosperous, and then you will have good success"* (Joshua 1:8 NKJV).

## Hang on to Correction with Humility

When God speaks to us, it is not always comfortable. Receiving correction is not comfortable, but humility will save our lives. Obedience is the key to victory. The children of Israel didn't want to receive correction from God because they were stiff-necked. They hardened their hearts against God in order to do their own thing. If we want to hear from God, then we need to have a humble and teachable spirit. This spirit will enable us to receive instruction and correction, that we may obey God and fulfill His plan.

We have to climb God's mountain for ourselves. If we are hungry, we will go up into His presence daily. That is where we will hear Him personally speak to us. Compromisers seek to please themselves. They want the preacher to be nice and make the Christian lifestyle easy, while making them feel good. Pleasers of men seek comfort. However, when God speaks to us, it is not always comfortable!

## Hang on to Hunger

Hearing God when He speaks is important to me, especially in times when I feel like I'm at the end of my rope. I hang on to the hunger for God's presence and I listen for Him to speak. That's how I keep focused on getting to the top of the mountain. I rest in God's presence until I hear from Him. I refuse to let anything distract me. When we stay in prayer and in His presence, He will speak to our hungry hearts.

I get excited when I read in the Bible about how Moses came to God, needing to hear from Him. For six days, Moses was so desperate for God that he would not leave until he heard from Him. Finally, God spoke to him: *"When Moses went up on the mountain, the cloud covered it, and the glory of the LORD settled on Mount Sinai. For six days the cloud covered the mountain, and on the seventh day the LORD called to Moses from within the cloud. To the Israelites the glory of the LORD looked like a consuming fire on top of the mountain"* (Exodus 24:15-17 NIV).

Moses persevered because he desired God's presence and depended on Him alone. When we are desperate to stay in God's presence, we will know God's will for our lives. When we are hungry for God we will say, "I can't make it without His presence; I'm desperate for Him."

Moses went into the midst of the cloud and up the mountain. He was on the mountain for forty days and nights (Exodus 24:18 NLT).

This is where God gave Moses the book of Genesis. When we get into God's presence like that, we'll have the will of God for our lives, churches, and ministries. We won't be like so many people who have been saved for ten years, yet still don't know what God has called them to do. They are still wandering around trying to figure out how to get out of debt. They are still trying to figure out if it is God's will to heal them or not.

It doesn't matter what we have been through or how old we are, we need to have a close relationship with God. When Moses got into the presence of God, He knew exactly what God wanted him to do for the rest of his life. Look how old he was. I'm not talking about a one-time, special event. I'm talking about a lifestyle of seeking God.

Just like Moses, I know that I can't make it without the presence of God. Moses said, *"If Your Presence does not go with us, do not bring us up from here. For how then will it be known that Your people and I have found grace in Your sight, except You go with us? So we shall be separate, Your people and I, from all the people who are upon the face of the earth"* (Exodus 33:15-16 NKJV).

## Don't Panic!
## Hang on to God's Peace

God's presence and peace go with us when we are Christians, but we have to recognize and hang on to them. I'm determined not to lose my peace in the storms. If it seems like I am losing my peace, I quickly get back into God's peace and hang on. When all else fails and everyone panics, God's peace which passes all understanding is inside of me, and His presence goes with me.

In 2009, I went to the doctor for a check-up. I had been feeling tired but didn't know why. They tested my blood and found that my hemoglobin was dangerously low and I was extremely anemic. I was immediately admitted to the hospital and began receiving blood transfusions.

The doctors and nurses were panicking and couldn't figure out how I was still carrying on normally. Yet, in the midst of all of this, the peace of God surrounded me and I stayed in faith. I didn't allow fear or the words of the doctors to put doubt in my mind. I just kept calling Jesus my healer and kept speaking to my blood.

I was in the hospital for a few days before my hemoglobin levels were high enough that I could go home. I started to eat a little meat again and began doing natural things to help build up my blood. I went back to the doctor and he said, "Your hemoglobin level is up and everything is normal. I'll see you in a year. I just want you to gain 15 pounds."

I said, "Whatever! You're skinnier than I am!"

He said, "That eating disorder is not trying to come back on you, is it?"

I said, "It tried, but I won't let it. I could skip a meal just like that and not even think about it. I have to make myself eat because the devil would love to try to get in and put that stupid anorexia on me again, but I won't allow him to do that."

You see, the devil will try to bring anything back to us that we have been set free from, but we don't have to receive it. If we stay focused on God's Word when everyone else panics, His peace will be inside of us. God's presence will go with us. When everyone else is confused, we will have the answers because we are walking with God and staying in His presence.

## Hang on to Your Personal Relationship with God

When everyone else is upset, we can have peace in the presence of God. The peace of God separates us from the world. In the world, life gets darker and darker with more disease, poverty, and despair, but God's presence makes us shine brighter and our lives are more peaceful.

The devil will bombard our minds with thoughts like, *You're going to die, you have a disease.* But the presence of God will make us say, "I'm healed, I'm free. It doesn't matter what's going on around me. It doesn't matter what I see. It doesn't matter how I feel. I don't need anybody else to be healed." According to 1 Peter 2:24, by the stripes of Jesus we were healed. That means that we are already healed, regardless of what our symptoms or circumstances may say.

Some people respond to the altar call and sinner's prayer and think that is all they need to do to be a Christian. But just saying a prayer every once in a while is not enough. We must seek a personal relationship with God in order to know and love Him. God is bigger than any religious routine.

God was pleased with Moses. He knew him by name and answered his prayers because he was a friend of God. The Bible says, *"And the Lord said to Moses, 'I will do the very thing you have asked, because I am pleased with you and I know you by name'"* (Exodus 33:17 NIV).

Can you imagine God doing something because you asked Him to do it? Can you imagine Him knowing your name? In other words, God was saying to Moses, "I'll do this because I like you Moses. I know you personally."

When we are hungry for God, nothing else matters more to us than walking with Him and staying in His presence. While the average person was squabbling about who squeezed the toothpaste wrong, Moses was hungry for the glory of God. Moses gave up everything—his will, his convenience, his agenda—in order to seek God. The average person is merely looking for someone to make him feel good. Moses' hunger is expressed in this scripture, *"And he said, 'Please, show me Your glory'"* (Exodus 33:18 NKJV).

Moses had a close relationship with God. Nothing else was more important to Moses than knowing God. He pursued the presence of God in every area of his life. Since Moses was totally dependent on God, favor came upon him in a special way. God's glory passed in front of him and God proclaimed His holy name. *"Then He said, 'I will make all My goodness pass before you, and I will proclaim the name of the Lord before you. I will be gracious to whom I will be gracious, and I will have compassion on whom I will have compassion.' But He said, 'You cannot see My face; for no man shall see Me, and live'"* (Exodus 33:19-20 NKJV).

## Hang on to Relying on Jesus

As we depend on Jesus in every area of our lives, He will cause us to reach the mountaintop. We have to be sure that we are putting our trust solely in Jesus to supply what we need in life. I had to depend solely on the Lord for my answer. I couldn't look to anyone else for my answer. I had to be full of faith. I couldn't rely on my husband's faith, my dad's faith, or anyone else's faith to get my miracle.

My late husband, Pastor Bobby, was a man of integrity. He was a great strength to me and had a deep understanding of the Word of God. I'll never forget when he passed away; I felt so alone. My whole world had just come down and bottomed out. If I didn't have my relationship with the Lord, I wouldn't have been able to make it.

I thank God that I have a relationship with Him. When we worship God and develop a personal relationship with Him, no matter what we're going through, His presence will carry us. He will help us. He will be our strength. He will stand by our side. He is our comfort and peace.

I had just had a physical before Bobby died. After five years with a transplant, they finally considered me normal. I got home and told Bobby, "Well, the doctor just closed the book and said I'm normal!" Bobby was doing something and looked up at me and said, "That's what I was waiting for; I knew it."

Then a month later, Bobby was dead. He knew that I was strong inside and didn't depend on him or my dad anymore. I had come to the realization that neither of them could get me out of the situations I faced. I realized that I had to rely solely on God.

I could no longer say to my dad, "The healing power of God flows through your hands. You lay hands on all these other people, but I'm your daughter. Lay hands on me. I believe I'm healed." My dad taught me to hit my knees and pray to God for an answer. I had to do it. I had to find God for myself. That's what you're going to have to do; you're going to have to find God for yourself. You're going to have to look to God as your source.

## Hang on to Walking in the Spirit

After my first husband died, I felt like my whole world had fallen apart and I didn't know how to start over alone. I went through a season of simply drawing closer to the Lord. He became my primary focus. Like Moses, I went up to draw closer to the presence of God. For six months, I stayed in my prayer closet. I worshiped God and found peace in His presence.

Moses "went up" into the presence of the Lord, which is exactly what we do through prayer. When we pray, we elevate ourselves and rise above our current circumstances. So for six months, I lifted myself up above loneliness and grief until I learned to live in that place of victory. Every day for hours, I would pray intensively in my prayer closet. I wouldn't come out except to clean up and even then, I would immediately return. Then, one day my dad called and said, "What are you doing?"

I said, "I am in my prayer closet."

He said, "You're going to get weird! Get out of your prayer closet!"

I said, "What?"

He explained, "You're going to get weird! You're not going to be one of those weird widows. Do you understand me? Get out of your prayer closet! Go to town!"

I needed to learn that life goes on. I had to find a balance between praying and living my life. My dad knew how to stay in the presence of God all the time, even as he went about his daily life. He wanted me to learn this too. I realized that God is always with me, so I can pray in the car or at the grocery store. I don't only have to pray in my prayer closet.

## Hang on to Passion for God

While worshipping God with hunger, the Holy Spirit will take us into God's presence. He will empower us with His glory. This is what happened to Moses (Exodus 33:21-23 NKJV).

Throughout the day, I always stop and take a few moments to worship Jesus and His presence comes upon me. I can be going along with my daily routine, but God's presence will flood me once I start worshipping Jesus. It doesn't matter what I'm going through, as long as I look to the Lord in the midst of my trials, He always gets me through. I raise my hands and surrender to the Lord. After ten or more times of saying, "I worship You, Jesus," the presence of the Lord will start to flood me. Tears start to form in my eyes, and I realize the situation doesn't matter because I can always go to Him.

Genuine worship is not a ritual. It's not based on how many times we raise our hands, kneel on the floor, stand up, or sit in a chair. Worship is heartfelt, spontaneous surrender. I love to worship God with my whole heart and feel His presence come on me.

If we lose our passion to worship God and just do it out of a routine without meaning it with our whole heart, then we won't be able to hang on to God's presence and peace when we go through great adversity or attack. Refuse to settle for man-made religion. We can be like Moses who asked for one thing—more of God's presence!

If we want our children to obey God, controlling them or demanding our way does not accomplish this. It's accomplished by showing them God's love. Everything is about His love. If we hunger and thirst for His presence, He'll give us whatever we need. We won't lack anything.

I refuse to get distracted by giving my passion to other things. I won't make God second place in my life; I choose to passionately seek Him first. I make true passion for Him my motivation for serving, whether I'm at home, on the job, or at church. We should worship God with a passion that flows from a pure heart and is accompanied by pure motives.

We won't be changed if we come to church as a spectator, simply to watch others enjoy God's presence. We have to come with the right motive. If our motive is to watch others enter into God's presence or to entertain our flesh, we won't get anything out of that service. That's why we get bored, become spiritually dry, and find ourselves stuck in a routine of religious performance, rather than a place of passionate surrender.

If we worship to please someone or to impress people, we will get bored. When we come for the right reason—to enjoy God's presence - we will receive His Word. I love to come into His presence with a pure heart, to participate in genuine worship for the purpose of delighting myself in the Lord. That's when He gives me the desires of my heart. Afterwards, I not only see the mountain path more clearly, but I'm able to keep climbing and fulfilling my destiny.

Out of hunger and a pure heart, Moses went up to see the glory of God. He was drawn to God's presence. He wanted to go where the glory cloud of God covered the mountain (Exodus 24:17). We can renew our passion for Jesus by worshipping God with all of our hearts.

Lift up your hands to God, surrender everything to Him and tell Him, "I love You, Jesus! I worship You!" Worship Him until His presence surrounds you. Then throughout the day, take time to worship and honor Him. That is how I hang on to God's peace. That same peace and presence of God will come on all of us as we worship Him.

# 2

# HANG ON TO FAITH

*"But without faith it is impossible to please him:*
*for he that cometh to God must believe that he is,*
*and that he is a rewarder of them*
*that diligently seek him"*

Hebrews 11:6

In order to climb the mountain, we have to hang on to faith in God's Word and step up (by that faith) into new heights. Faith is a powerful weapon God gave us that we might live a victorious life.

### Hang on to Stubborn Faith

When I was attacked by the devil, I not only resisted the devil, but I also tightened my grip on faith. That's how I received God's benefits. I was attacked several times with low potassium, but I refused to let the devil kill me. I stepped out in faith to get my miracle.

I nearly died twice from low potassium. I would wake up, not knowing if my potassium level was going to go up or down. When your potassium level goes down, your muscles become so weak they are unable to work. Low potassium can even affect your heart. My potassium would get so low that I couldn't walk.

One time my late husband, Pastor Bobby, and I were driving from Alabama to Cleveland in our Volkswagen hatchback. I lay down in the back seat and went to sleep. When we arrived Bobby said, "Okay little Zona, it is time to get out." But when I tried to get out of the car, I realized I couldn't move my arms or legs. I couldn't move anything. My body felt lifeless from my arms down. Bobby had to carry me around the next day.

We were going to move to Kingston, Tennessee, so Bobby carried me and said, "We're going to go hunt an apartment in Kingston." Every apartment building we came to, he had to get out of the car and come to my side. Then he would pick me up and bring me to the apartment. We would meet the manager and he would carry me inside. Then he would carry me back to the car and we would go to another building.

We stopped at Dairy Queen to eat, but I couldn't use my arms to feed myself. Bobby had to sit me down first and then get my food. He cut it for me and fed me. The next day we were going to go water skiing. That morning, Bobby got up and told me that he was going to get the boat ready. I said, "I'm going to stay here."

He replied, "Go with me. I will carry you."

I told him, "No, I'm going to stay here."

I made everybody in our household leave because I didn't want anybody to stay with me. While lying in my bed, I said, "Okay devil, you're a liar. I'm going to walk by the end of this day. I'm going to walk in Jesus' name. My arms are going to move in the name of Jesus." I was still in bed, but my arms gained a little bit more strength.

I decided to make my body work, so I rolled out of bed and fell flat on the floor. That hurt, but I knew that if I could get my arms around the leg of the dresser and my foot around the leg of the bed, I could stretch my arms and pull myself back up. I exercised by stretching out my arm and pulling myself back up.

I must have done that thirty times before my arm got some strength back in it. Then, I did the same exercise using the other arm about thirty times. I got some strength back in my arms and kept confessing, "In Jesus' name, my muscles are normal. I bind you, low potassium, in Jesus' name."

I had already eaten a banana and drank some orange juice to put potassium back in my body, but my legs still wouldn't work. Finally, I had enough strength in my arms to pull myself into the kitchen. I grabbed the handle on a bottom drawer in the kitchen and with my right hand, I pulled myself up. Then I used my left arm and pushed myself further up. After that, I was able to take my right arm and place it on the counter.

I tried to let go of the counter, but I would fall. Over and over again, I did that whole routine by faith, speaking the Word and employing stubborn determination. All day long, I didn't stop. By five o'clock when Bobby came in the house, I was in the living room chair. I looked at him and said, "Bobby, look!" Then I walked to him.

Because I took authority over the enemy's strategy and used the weapon of the Word, combined with the name of Jesus, I started walking again, against all odds. It's time for all of us to climb the mountain and receive all that God has for us. There's power in taking a step of faith and not giving up.

# Hang on to Diligence
# to Reach the Top

Climbing a mountain, just like our walk in Christ, takes diligence. When climbing a high mountain, a person has to be diligent to reach the mountaintop. He has to make a decision and set his goal on the mountaintop. Then he goes forward and never changes direction or retreats. He walks by faith, believing that he will reach the top. Even when the mountain seems impossible to climb, he keeps a single-mind that he is going higher.

I like to follow this same attitude of diligence to reach my goal in Christ. The Bible tells us to be single-minded and diligent in our walk with the Lord. That means we must go forward and stay focused on our goal to fulfill our call in life. My dad calls this stubborn faith, when you find a promise of God and hold on to it—no matter what happens. He did this when he was cursing the growths on my body and when he was standing in the gap for me. He held on with stubborn faith until it came to pass.

I was thirty-eight years old when I finally sold out to God. Ever since then, I've been diligent as I walk by faith to go higher, especially when going through adversity. I decided I would never go through the routine of everyday life functioning on a low level.

People may admire consistency, but if we do the same old thing every day, we are going to get the same old results. I made a decision that I was going to overcome the physical problems I was going through. No matter what happened, I set my goal on God's best—to walk in health and victory. In order to reach the top, we have to change and do what we have not done before.

If we truly desire to walk in abundant life, then we need to let go of living below God's standard. We have to say, "Wait a minute! I don't have to wonder if God is going to do what He said He would." We can't say that we are going higher and then allow the devil to play with our minds and make us quit. We have to be determined not to give up. We have to decide that we will not give in to his lies. We must stay focused on God's Word, and His Word alone!

If our goal is to mine for gold, then we must first start to cut through the earth's surface and move beyond the norm. We need to make a decision to dig deeper and stay with it until we see results. We have to put action to our faith. That is when we will start to receive the benefits and results of the gold found in God's Word.

A diligent person does not just say that he believes God's Word, he takes action. The Bible says, *"The soul of a lazy man desires, and has nothing; but the soul of the diligent shall be made rich"* (Proverbs 13:4 NKJV). The decision to be diligent will make us rich in more areas than just finances. Those who are diligent will move beyond the lies of the enemy and receive God's victory in every area of their lives.

## Hang on — Don't Panic

In this hour, many panic when everything else fails. Instead of looking at our failures, we need to keep our confidence in God's Word, worship God, and pray until we overflow with His presence. That's how we let the peace of God rule in us. It doesn't matter how bad a situation looks, if we keep our mind on Jesus, He will keep us in perfect peace.

## Hang on to Hearing God

I want to hear from God myself. Unfortunately, many would rather hear from someone else who heard from God rather than spending the time to hear from God for themselves. They want to hear a word that someone else gave, so they wind up seeking men instead of God.

Our society wants to see someone else do something because we don't want to do it ourselves. People would rather watch baseball or football than get involved in playing these sports. Likewise, many prefer to watch church rather than participate in church. We have to expect to hear from God for ourselves before He will show us things to come, give instruction, share His heart with us, and empower us to fulfill our purpose.

When we have been in God's presence, people will see evidence of God's character in us and will want what we have. There should be an atmosphere of expectation and hunger around us. We should expect great things to happen. Then, wherever we go, His presence will be with us and flow through us.

## Hang on to Your Destiny Mindset

Climbing a high mountain is not about comfort. It takes great effort, determination, steadfastness, and a willingness to do what we haven't done before. Living for Jesus is not about comfort either; it's about surrendering our will. We do this by laying down all selfishness and deciding to win souls and follow Christ. To go higher, we must totally surrender saying, "*... not My will, but Yours, be done*" (Luke 22:42 NKJV).

In America, many want comfort. This is more important to them than God's presence. They don't want to change and are consequently stuck in a rut of spiritual lethargy and religious performance. They want to attend a church where they can just sit in the pew, a church where they can watch from a distance without being challenged to step forward and participate. Many say, "Well, I've been supporting you for years. I'm tired of serving." But this isn't the stance that Jesus took. He said that He came to serve. He is still our example today.

To go up higher, we need to keep a servant's heart. God can't do great and mighty things through those who are lazy and content with doing nothing, those who are comfortable with their disobedience to God's Word. Yet, many wonder why they are miserable, struggling, and broke. This isn't the life God intended for us to live.

## Hang on to God's Word and Resist the Devil's Tricks

I refuse to succumb to the devil's tricks. Instead, I hang on to God's Word. The devil has many tricks he uses to get us to not believe God's Word and will for our lives. They are tricks to get us off our course. These distractions will cause us to lose faith in God's Word and quit climbing. They will also cause us to quit praying, worshiping, and obeying God.

That's why I have set my eyes on reaching the top. No matter what happens, I hang onto God's Word because nothing is impossible with God. In everything we do, we have to set our goal on Heaven and get back to climbing that mountain. Put Jesus and His Word first.

Let me expose some tricks the devil uses to get us off course. First and foremost, the devil will lie to us because he is the father of lies. When a lie of the devil comes to our minds, immediately we must resist it. That is the key to hanging on to faith.

The devil tries to distract us with excuses and tell us why we can't climb our mountain and do God's will for our lives. When those thoughts come, we must do the opposite and keep climbing by saying what God's Word says. That's why I am determined to know what the Bible says, so I can believe it and do it. I talk to God personally because I believe the Bible says I can. According to James 4:8, we can draw close to God, and He'll draw near to us.

The devil will try to make us believe that we can't hear God. That's why we must know what the Word says concerning hearing God's voice. When we know what the Word says, we will recognize the devil's lies. When the devil tries to convince us that we can't hear God for ourselves, we can stand upon John 10:27: *"My sheep hear My voice, and I know them, and they follow me"* (NKJV).

The devil comes to steal our peace and tries to convince us that we aren't free to receive God's presence. That is nothing but a lie from hell. He will try to persuade us to listen to our flesh, instead of reading or confessing God's Word. He will try to trick us into thinking that we are tired and if we listen to him, we will fall asleep or do something else rather than seek God's presence. I am thankful that my dad taught me to resist the devil. The truth makes us free and keeps us free from the lies of the devil.

The devil wants to make us believe that God doesn't hear us when we pray and that He won't answer our prayers. That is a lie from hell. When that thought comes, we should reject it outright. Without faith, it is impossible to please God. Faith believes that God is a rewarder of those that seek Him. I tell the devil that he is a liar and remind him what God's Word says. I tell him that Hebrews 11:6 says when I seek God, He will reward me.

I hold on to God's Word. This gives me confidence that if I ask God anything that agrees with His Word, He won't only hear me, but He will also give me whatever I desire of Him. The Word of God will erase all unbelief. Tell the devil what the Bible says. Say the following verse: *"And this is the confidence that we have in him, that, if we ask any thing according to his will, he heareth us: And if we know that he hear us, whatsoever we ask, we know that we have the petitions that we desired of him"* (1 John 5:14-15).

Faith speaks to sickness, disease, problems, financial lack, adversity, and attacks on our lives. It enables us to use our God-given authority with no doubt. This makes situations conform to God's will.

## Hang on to Life!

I made a decision that I would live and not die. I had to make the right decision or it could have cost me my life. When we hear wisdom, we need to be quick to listen. We live in a body and if we don't take care of our body, we won't live very long. The devil has tried to kill me numerous times but whatever he purposed for bad, God has always turned for good. Whenever the enemy attacks me, I hear my dad's voice speaking life-giving words.

My dad has repeatedly said, "Zona, your first reaction to any diagnosis is either life or death. You can't get weak and you cannot act weak. Faith is not weak. It is strong. You have to stay strong. You can't quit. Faith without action is dead. You have to do it!"

When doctors gave me thirty days to live, I said, "Dad! You pray for me! You have God's healing power flowing through your hands. Put your hands on my head and I will be healed. I believe it!" He did, but nothing happened.

After that, I went to my husband and said, "You're the head of the house. Run the devil off of your wife!" He tried to, but the devil didn't go.

Then the Lord said, "Zona! There is no man who is going to write a book about this. There is no man who is going to take credit for this. This is between you and Me. If you make the right decisions, you will live. If you make the wrong decisions, you will come home early, which is not My will. The only way you can carry the mantle of this ministry is to make the right decisions. Quit looking to your dad for everything."

## Hang on to a Step of Faith

When I felt I was at the end of my rope, I wouldn't quit or give up. I wouldn't let go of my faith, but instead did the opposite and took a step of faith. Let me give you an example of how I applied the Word and took a step of faith.

I would go to the bathroom when my kidneys weren't working at all and close the door. Then I would take a glass of water and pour it into the commode saying, "Thank You, Jesus, that my kidneys are functioning normally." I would then proceed to tear off toilet tissue, put it in the commode, and flush it. Afterwards, I would walk over to the sink, wash and dry my hands, and then walk out as if everything was fine. I did this five or six times every day for a year and a half. As a step of faith, I was calling those things that be not as though they were.

The Bible tells us that God called those things that be not as though they were. Before Abraham had a son, God called him the father of many nations (Romans 4:17). Abraham believed and began to call things that were not as though they were already done.

When there was no possible way for Abraham and Sarah to have children, Abraham believed that he would become what God told him. He believed that all things are possible with God. His faith was not dependent on circumstances, but was based totally on what God had said. Our miracle will come as we say what God says, not by talking about our problems (Romans 4:18).

Faith refuses to be weak. It does not even consider that our circumstances are impossible; it sees all things as possible with God. When Abraham came to the end of his rope, he would have failed if he had weak faith. The Bible says, however, that he was not weak in faith. He was a hundred years old, and yet he wouldn't consider his body too old to have a son. He wouldn't even consider that his wife was too old to have children (Romans 4:19).

Faith is not moved by our circumstances or by what we feel or see. Abraham hung on by not changing or moving away from his faith in what God's Word said. He hung on to God's promise by not staggering through unbelief. He was strong in faith, giving glory to God. That is how Abraham hung on—with strong faith.

We have to stop complaining about the negative report and continually give glory to God for our miracle. Abraham hung on by being fully persuaded that God would do what He promised (Romans 4:20-21). He was not up one day and down the next. He held on by holding steadfastly to God. Like Abraham, we need to be fully persuaded of what God has promised, speaking those promises and never changing our confession.

Abraham wasn't affected by the contrary circumstance of his old age. If we want to have our breakthrough, we can never put our faith in a bad report, our feelings, symptoms, or the words of people. Only believe and confess what God's Word says about your situation.

Miracles happen when we refuse to waver from what God has said (James 1:6). Abraham's testimony was written so we could follow his example of faith. It was written for our sake, to encourage us to be fully persuaded and believe and confess God's promises until we see the manifested results (Romans 4:23-24).

## Hang on by Being a Doer

I couldn't hang on by only listening to other people's success stories; I had to act myself. I chose to be a doer of the Word. In order to be a doer of the Word, I had to get to a higher spiritual plane. By faith, I stepped up and did what God said.

Maybe you have heard about blessings that others have received and wondered why you haven't received them. God didn't call you to be a spectator, only listening to the great things that God has done for others. Instead, He has called you to walk by faith and do the same things that Jesus did. Many have heard of preachers who saw, heard, went, and did, but they have never seen, heard, gone, or did themselves. We have become a nation of spectators. To change, we have to step up and reach the mountaintop.

Some say, "I had a desire to do so many things for the Lord." I tell them, "You have to get out of the bleachers and get into the game. I have a desire for you to be someone who not only hears about the great things that God has done, but who gets right in the middle of what God is doing. God wants participants, not spectators. That is God's desire for you. Don't settle for just a little bit of what God has for you. If you get all that God has for you, you will always win and never lose!"

When we get down on our knees and say, "Father," He will respond to us by saying, "Yes, son," or "Yes, daughter." We can have what God has prepared for us, because we are children of God. We can be confident in knowing that God loves us and that He has already given us victory through Jesus.

Many people exclude themselves from doing what they really want to do. They don't believe they have what it takes to do what God has called them to do. People can easily make excuses and say, "I have always wanted to do what God said, but I never could."

Others give excuses like, "Oh, I don't have the time," "I don't have the finances," "I'm too young," "I'm too old," "I am not strong enough," "I'm not talented enough," "I am not trained," or "I don't have that kind of experience." We can all make an excuse and stay where we are, or we can change and go higher. All of us have something we can allow to exclude us from the higher life, but the truth is, we can do all things through Christ who gives us the strength. "All things" means everything. We cannot allow an excuse to stop us from going where we need to go.

I had to look at the Word of God and just do it, expecting God to fulfill His Word. The Lord continually reminds me of His Word. *"For it is God who works in you both to will and to do for His good pleasure"* (Philippians 2:13 NKJV). God is effectually working in us and through us to do things that produce results.

## Hang on by Fighting Back

We have to hang on by fighting back the thoughts the devil puts in our minds. He tries to stop us from obtaining our victory; we have to resist his lies. The devil will try to discourage us from stepping out to do what it takes to fulfill our destiny. He wants to steal God's Word and plan from us so we won't fulfill the destiny we were created to fulfill.

The Bible says, *"The thief does not come except to steal, and to kill, and to destroy. I have come that they may have life, and that they may have it more abundantly"* (John 10:10 NKJV). We can't accept any lies of the devil. We have to keep our minds made up to step out and do what God has put on our hearts. We have to refuse to entertain his lies and continue to step out and do the opposite, obeying God. When thoughts come in our mind that are contrary to God's Word, we must be bold to counterattack with the truth of the Word and take every thought captive to the obedience of Christ Jesus our Lord.

If we don't fight back when the enemy attacks, we won't win. But God has made us to be winners so we have to use our authority against the devil. I encourage you to just step out and act according to the Word. You will reap great blessings, fulfill your destiny, and reach the mountaintop. Be willing to step out and do something that is new; otherwise, you will never have what you need to get the job done.

## Hang on by Doing What You Didn't Do Before

Refuse to stay in the status quo. Rise above it by doing what you haven't done before. When we do what we haven't done before, we will have unwavering faith that expects God to show up. To climb to the mountaintop, our faith has to be alive, not dead. We aren't living by faith if we stay in the norm and get accustomed to just getting by. We can't have God's kind of faith by being normal. Rise above by having your eyes set on the mountaintop. See your promise, speak your promise, and act by faith in God's Word alone!

I love how my dad taught me to step out by faith. The first time I was taking up an offering, and there was a sea of people. My dad said, "Zona, I want you to receive the offering tonight."

I said, "What? Me?" I bent down and said, "I have never received an offering before."

He said, "I want you to receive the offering tonight."

I said, "I've never received an offering before, Dad." I couldn't let the people in the crowd know that I was flipping out inside.

My dad said, "Little Zona, bend down here and let me talk to you for a minute."

I said, "What?"

He replied, "Faith is doing something you have never done, but you go ahead and do it. Don't let anyone know that you don't know what you are doing. Now get your Scripture together!"

My knees were knocking; I thought I was going to throw up. I had never felt like that before. I felt that way because I had made receiving the offering into a bigger issue than it actually was. That's what the devil likes to do.

## Hang on by Expecting God to Show up

Faith not only says, "I worship You, Jesus," but it also expects God to show up. Expect Him to show up when you say, "I worship You, Jesus. I worship You, Lord. I worship You! I worship You, Jesus." When

I worship God, I expect Him to show up. By worshipping God out of hunger, there is an expectation that God will show up. Too many Christians don't expect God to show up, and that's one reason why they aren't walking in victory.

The only reason we experience defeat in our lives is because our expectation is not where it's supposed to be. This happens if we aren't worshipping God long enough to build up our faith.

## Hang on! Don't Let Worry Come on You

With anything we try to overcome, the devil wants to magnify the problem and cause us to worry. We have to trust the Lord. It's just like the television ministry that we are doing. Before we started, I felt like a nervous wreck. I thought, *Oh man, this is not going to go well. They don't know me. They are just going to want to hear Brother Norvel.*

Then, I thought that the viewers were going to call on the phone and say, "Why do we need her on there? Why can't we just have Brother Norvel?" But my dad told me that if either of those things happened, I was supposed to ignore them. That's how I learned to climb my mountain. I thank God that my dad taught me wisdom in how to climb my mountain by faith, ignoring pressure, fear, worry, and anxiety. He taught me that there are no big "I's" and little "you's" in ministry; we have to work together.

I am so thankful he taught me this principle of having a willing heart. He told me, "You are the only one who can do it, but you have to be willing and not get offended." When I was obedient to do this, people began to come up to me at the grocery store or drug store to tell me they saw me on TV and were blessed.

God began to give me His heart when I said, "Lord Jesus, let me have Your heart first. Let me continue to be humble and have the heart and compassion that my dad has." We had something happen at the ministry and I didn't react to it at all. I said, "Dad, I want you to lay hands on me. I want you to continue to pray for me, because I am so proud of the way I didn't react to this situation." As he laid his hands on me, he said, "I thank You, Lord, that Zona has calmness, except when it comes to dealing with the devil."

I was tested when a staff member suddenly left the ministry. We were in the middle of a big project and I only had a two-hour notice that this staff member was leaving. I asked my staff member, "Why are you leaving?"

He replied, "God has called us to go back home."

I responded, "Okay, when?"

He said, "Tonight."

I said, "Oh, well, praise the Lord."

I went to my office the next day and sat there for a few minutes by myself and prayed, "Lord, I'm not going to panic. I'm not going to get upset. This is between You and me. I'm not going to get nervous." At that moment, I decided that if everybody walked out on me, it didn't matter. I would say, "Lord, it is You and me. You're going to have to send the right one. It's between You and me. You send the right one for this position and we'll get through this."

That is exactly what I had to do. God does not bless nervous faith. When I made my decision, nobody else got nervous. I didn't react badly. I didn't let oppression come on me. Nervousness wasn't able to overtake me because I didn't let my heart get involved. Before this time, I had been through situations in which my heart was ripped out.

When people lie to us and don't respect us enough to keep their word, we have to stay focused on God. If we allow other people's actions to affect us, it will rip out our hearts. I thank God that my dad taught me how to cast my cares on the Lord and not allow myself to be oppressed.

When I refused to be nervous, I thought, *I have really moved to a higher spiritual plane. People don't bother me anymore. I'm not being ruled by people.* Praise God! That is something to rejoice about! This same thing can happen to any of us, but we don't have to react when the devil attacks. Instead, we can choose to live in the peace of the Lord.

# 3

# CUT THE ROPE OF COMPROMISE

*"And be renewed in the spirit of your mind;*
*And that ye put on the new man, which after God is created in*
*righteousness and true holiness.*
*Neither give place to the devil."*

Ephesians 4:23-24, 27

We need to make sure we are hanging on to the right kind of rope, one that will hold us when we climb the mountain of the Lord. If we hang on to the rope of compromise, we will find it weak and powerless, unable to hold us when we are at the end of our rope. Holding on to compromise is like holding on to string instead of the heavy-duty rope of God's Word.

We can cut the rope of compromise by cutting away anything that is not of God in our hearts and lives. We can do this by renewing our mind with the Word of God. Today in many churches, there is compromise to the flesh, sin, and works of darkness. Instead of giving room to the anointing and God's Word, many yield to the flesh and the devil. We have to cut the rope of compromise.

## Hang on to God's Direction

We can't climb a mountain if we compromise by doing our own thing. We need to hang on to God's direction and no matter what happens, stay with His plan and let nothing distract us. If God has led us to do something, He is not going to change His mind.

The devil will try to persuade us that we need to go somewhere else or do something else other than what God's calling entails. That is called compromise and will get us in trouble. Obey God by staying on course with the plan He has given you.

I've seen this many times, both as a pastor and as the dean of students at our Bible College. Church members and students say that God called them to come to our ministry, but when times get tough or they come under attack, they give in to compromise and decide to leave. Some even air their dirty laundry and then come to me and say, "God has called me to go to the church down the street."

I simply respond by saying, "Ok, praise the Lord!" There is no point in arguing or disagreeing with them because they believe God spoke to them. Yet God knew there would be attacks before He told them to come to our ministry. When God calls us to go somewhere or do something, He will give us the grace and provision we need to follow through. But we can't give in to compromise.

Often these people will come back a year or so later and want to meet with me. They will say, "I just hear voices and I don't know what to do. My mind is confused."

I answer, "Really? Does the church you attend cast out devils?"

They answer, "Well, they take a person in the back room."

I boldly say, "Jesus doesn't have any 'back room' ministries."

Afterwards, they cowardly and softly respond by saying, "Well, I just need you to break the power of the devil over me."

I question, "Where are you going to church?" They respond, giving me the name of such-and-such church. Then I say, "I'm not going to break the power of the devil over you. You need to go to your pastor."

I am not popular, but neither am I falling for the ways of the world. I don't steal sheep. I would rather have five people whom God sent to my church, than five hundred people I stole because I bought their dinner or gave them twenty dollars.

## Hang on to the Right Decision

Making right decisions is the key to our freedom. I refuse to die in the wilderness of compromise. In the wilderness, we must hear and heed the voice of the Lord. When I was going through dialysis, I needed to hear the voice of the Lord. Jesus said to me, "You're getting tired and I can't meet you where your faith is if you get tired. Don't look to the right or the left; just look straight ahead. Don't look at the dialysis machine. If you start looking at the machine, you are going to get tired."

The Lord impressed me to take a blanket with me and cover myself up the whole time I was at dialysis. I would stick my arm out from underneath the blanket for the treatment, while listening to teaching tapes or worship music. I looked like I was under a teepee, but I only left a little space open so I could breathe.

After dialysis, I would get back up and teach faith. That was the hardest thing I ever did in my life. I felt like a fraud for teaching faith. That is how the devil made me feel. The devil did everything he could to make me quit.

I had to get my mind and emotions under control. I couldn't think about my blood going through the machine. I couldn't let the words of the enemy take root in my heart and mind, or else I would have died.

For two years, I didn't drink anything. I had to watch everything I ate because it might have water in it. I had to get my water through frozen grapes and strawberries. Between treatments, you can't consume over 2.2 pounds of fluid when you are on dialysis. I was determined to follow the procedures of dialysis. The more fluid you have to get off, the more your heart is in jeopardy. I was their model patient. I didn't go over the 2.2 pounds, except once.

I would watch people eat and drink and wish I could be like them. I would even watch their throat move up and down as they swallowed, and I tried to remember what it felt like. But I had to keep walking in faith. I had to keep control of, not just my body through what I ate and drank, but also my mind and emotions through the Word of God. I couldn't afford to give in to pity or "what-if's," if I wanted to live!

## Hang on! Refuse to Quit

We have to cut off all thoughts about giving up and quitting our climb. I made a decision that no matter how bad my circumstances were, I would never give up and quit the climb into God's will for my life. I made a decision that my relationship with Jesus meant more to me than anything or anyone.

I owned a fitness center for over twelve years. Every year, I would have to go to exercise clinics for training and certification. These exercise clinics consisted of long days of working out, and I would get tired and ache all over. I would have thoughts of quitting. I would think, *Maybe I should stop right here, go back to my motel room, and just camp out.* But something would hit me and say, "You are halfway to the top. You are about to conquer this thing!" In like manner, this is what the right pastor will do in our lives. He or she will encourage us to reach the top.

## Hang on — Finish Your Assignment

If we hang on to God's best for our lives and don't compromise, we will always graduate to the next level. While climbing our mountain, we need correction and instruction. We need the wisdom of team leaders who have experience and know the best way for us to succeed. If we are humble enough to receive that correction, it will keep us from destruction.

We need to receive correction when our pastor or leader gives it to us. We should be thankful when they give us correction to help us become victorious and successful in our climb to the mountaintop. The Bible says, *"Obey those who rule over you, and be submissive, for they watch out for your souls, as those who must give account. Let them do so with joy and not with grief, for that would be unprofitable for you*" (Hebrews 13:17 NKJV).

If we receive correction and thereby hold on to God's best for our lives, God will promote us. A pastor is accountable to put God's Word first in both his life and ministry. He must not compromise by being a people pleaser.

## Don't Hang on to Excuses for Your Problems

In order to receive God's best, we must refuse to hang out in the lowland of excuses, problems, and discouragement. We need to get into God's presence and obey Jesus. As we do what He told us to do, He will cause our ministries to keep going upward.

Years ago when this ministry was started, negative people said, "Your ministry is not going to last. It is just a flash in the pan. It is just faith for a moment." People thought it would be a temporary thing and wouldn't last. But it does not matter what people say; it only matters what Jesus says. That is what counts.

People were amazed when we were still going five, ten, fifteen, and twenty years later. This ministry has been helping people for over thirty years now, and we're not slowing down. We will be here another thirty years if Jesus tarries!

Since we are climbing up the mountain of God, New Life Bible College and New Life Bible Church will still be going when Jesus comes back. We will not entertain excuses for living in the valley. We will not settle for life in the lowlands. We will not hang out in debt, poverty, depression, and discouragement.

Moses received the Word of God, and he was in a cloud of glory for forty days and forty nights. God was dealing with him. Notice what the people said to Moses. *"Then they said to Moses, 'You speak with us, and we will hear; but let not God speak with us, lest we die'"* (Exodus 20:19 NKJV).

If we do not follow spiritual disciplines, something else will take the place that God is supposed to have in our lives. Some of these disciplines include reading and studying God's Word, attending church, praying, worshipping, and getting into His presence. All of these disciplines lead to a successful climb up the mountain.

During the week, if we don't want to take the time to praise the Lord, help somebody, or seek and hear God, something else will take His place in our lives. It is awesome to hear great words and messages, but it is not enough to only hear the Word. To overcome and live a victorious life, we have to practice what we hear.

## Hang on to Self-Control

I chose to cut the rope of compromise and climb the mountain with self-control. It takes self-control to climb the mountain of God and do what God tells us to do. I won't let the devil steal my health. I do what it takes to stay healthy.

Once, I had growths on my body, but thank God, I now have overcome and don't have those growths any longer. For twelve and a half years, I had anorexia and bulimia, but I refuse to give the devil room to let it come back on me. At one time, I almost killed myself taking sixty laxatives a day. But today, everything in my body functions normally. I refuse to give room to the lies of the devil.

Sometimes the devil will come during meals and say, "You can't eat that. Don't eat that." I will just cram the food in my mouth in opposition to his lies. My doctor said, "You are a very strict person. You are very diligent and you have a lot of will power. I can tell that about you. Once you make your mind up about something, you are going to do it come hell or high water."

And that's the truth! I refuse to let my body or my flesh do what it wants to do, whenever it wants to do it. We have to control our flesh and not allow it to control our lives.

## Hang on to Being an Example for Your Children to Follow

If we don't compromise to sin, our children will follow our example. We have to live a godly life because the Bible teaches us that if we set an example for our children and raise them up in the way they should go, they will not depart from it.

My dad lived a godly life while I was growing up. He didn't bring women or anything ungodly in the house. He had the money to go on cruises and meet women, but instead he chose to walk in obedience to the Lord. Don't get me wrong, my dad was definitely tempted. Women would knock at our door, but I would answer. They would come to the book table and I would think, *Are you kidding me?*

I went on a trip with my dad that I will never forget. A lady called my dad when we were packing to leave and I answered the telephone, "Hello?" She asked, "May I speak to Brother Norvel?"

I replied, "Hold on," and gave the phone to my dad.

He said, "Hello?"

She told him, "I am ready to go."

He asked, "I beg your pardon?"

She replied, "I am ready to go."

We were getting ready to head back to Cleveland, so he said, "I am glad you are getting ready to go. Where are you going?"

She replied, "With you. I am going back to Cleveland. God told me I was going to marry you."

He told her, "You flaky thing! You are not going back to Cleveland with me!"

My dad was a good man and never brought women home. He never cursed or drank. He lived a holy life and made sure no one could ever question his name or his character. I still follow the example he gave about being a Christian. He taught me to be a person of compassion, wisdom and integrity. I want to be a good example of both for my daughter, as well as for the students who come to New Life Bible College. I want to be a living example of how to be real and how to walk in love, forgiveness and faith in every situation.

# 4

# CUT THE ROPE OF DISTRACTION

*"Brethren, I count not myself to have apprehended: but this one*
*thing I do, forgetting those things which are behind, and reaching*
*forth unto those things which are before. I press toward the mark*
*for the prize of the high calling of God in Christ Jesus."*

Philippians 3:13-14

## Hang on by Forgetting
## What is Behind You

When people have been through things, it is easy for them to hang on to past mistakes, hurts, or even successes. But we can't move forward if we are still looking back. We have to let go of everything behind us.

I had to let go of my past. I would be stuck in a rut if I hung on to anything that wasn't moving me forward. Living off past successes or allowing past failures to stop us will hinder our focus from climbing higher.

We can't afford to focus on other things. Distractions come to get us off track and make us miss God's best for our lives. It doesn't matter what happens, we are blessed when we focus on fulfilling God's will for our lives. We have to keep going regardless of the circumstances around us. We must focus on our goals, letting go of our past and looking at what is ahead of us.

We must choose to forget what is behind and press on to the high call of Christ Jesus. One way we can do this is by aligning our thoughts and attitudes with the Word of God. We need to get His Word in us and let it fill every part of us so we won't live by what we see, hear or feel. Pursue Him daily and go higher, from glory to glory. When climbing a mountain, if we allow things to distract us, we can easily stumble, slip, and fall.

# Hang on to
# Fulfilling Your Destiny

We fulfill our destinies by obeying what God says and not getting distracted. Many Christians get distracted by the daily requirements of life and set aside their destinies in order to pursue natural agendas. When students attend our Bible College, they attend because they heard God's call on their lives. They come to receive solid Biblical teaching, develop discipline, and fulfill their God-given destiny. But just like all Christians, they undergo great attacks. This is because the devil will try to stop those who seek to obey the call of God.

I've seen so many students who were excited about attending Bible College, but soon, the devil began to throw things in their path to distract them. The devil will bring in problems at home, financial hardship, and anything else he can in order to get our focus off what God has called us to do and where He called us to be.

The devil is a thief and he wants to take us out of God's will for our lives. The Bible says in Romans 11:29 that the calling of God is without repentance. That means that God doesn't change His mind about what He has called us to do. Even when times get tough, God's destiny is still true for our lives. He doesn't look at our circumstances and say, "Oh, I didn't know that it would be difficult. This problem really surprised Me so I guess we'll need to find another destiny for you." That's a lie from the devil that people choose to believe because it is easier than dealing with the situation they are facing. God will give us the grace and provision for every obstacle we face. We have to make up our minds that we are not going to quit, give in, or give up until we have fulfilled everything God has called us to do.

## Hang on by Putting Jesus First

When I felt I was at the end of my rope and there seemed to be no way to climb the mountain, I hung on by focusing on Jesus. Distractions come, not only to direct our eyes *onto* something, but also to take our eyes *off* of something. The devil brings distractions to keep us focused on his lies. Even more importantly, his distractions are intended to take our eyes off of Jesus. Our victory only comes through Jesus, so we must stay focused on Him.

Moses went up the mountain and into God's presence. He was only gone for forty days before the Israelites concluded that they had to make their own idol. They compromised because they didn't want to have a personal relationship with God. If we don't know God, we won't be able to trust Him and we will rely on someone else's knowledge of

Him to get us by. We can't rely on someone else's relationship with God; we need to have our own personal relationship with Him. That way we won't be tempted to compromise. Compromise opens the door to having a deceived, stubborn, and rebellious heart (Exodus 32:1 NKJV).

The Israelites lost their focus on the word that God had said and the promises He had given them regarding the Promised Land. They focused on the temporary pleasures of sin, which turned their hearts against God. As a result, they became hard hearted, stiff-necked, rebellious, and disobedient to God's call and vision.

We are living in the last days, so it is very easy to get our priorities out of order. When our priorities shift off of God and onto anything else, we begin exalting these things in our lives, just like the children of Israel who made their own idol because they thought they knew best what they needed.

When people put their own plans and desires over obedience and a personal relationship with God, they start to think that they can figure things out on their own. Before they know it, they are missing church services, not praying regularly, not giving, and not plugging into the Word. Instead of a personal relationship with the Lord, their idol soon becomes money, family, friends, sports, movies or anything else on which they put importance. They make these things their first love and end up replacing the position that God used to hold in their lives.

Years ago, I did this by allowing my fitness center to become my god. For the first three years, I was there almost every day. On Sundays, I would go in and clean the fitness center and all of the equipment in detail. After years of hard work, I finally paid off all the fitness center equipment. Then suddenly, disaster struck! The telephone rang and the person who called exclaimed, "Your business is on fire!"

I replied, "Whatever!" and hung up the phone. I thought somebody was playing a prank on me. They called back and insisted, "Your business is on fire, Zona! We are serious!" So I got in my car and drove into town. As I came to the bridge, I saw the black smoke. It seemed like the whole town came out to see my business burn.

I pulled up and it was like the parting of the Red Sea. Everyone was watching as I walked up because they wanted to see how I was going to react. I just looked at it and thought, *I have fireproof file cabinets. If I can get a fireman to go in there and retrieve my file cabinets, I can start over.*

After the fire was extinguished, they went in to see if there was anything that could be salvaged. They discovered that the fire had gone completely around my file cabinets and my stereo. All of my files and my music were completely fine; they weren't damaged at all! You can't ever quit. You have to have that mindset. It has to be rooted and grounded inside of you.

## Hang on to Righteousness

In these last days, if we don't keep walking in righteousness before God, our hearts will become deceived, hard, deaf, and blind to the things of God. *"But know this, that in the last days perilous times will come: For men will be lovers of themselves, lovers of money, boasters, proud, blasphemers, disobedient to parents, unthankful, unholy, unloving, unforgiving, slanderers, without self-control, brutal, despisers of good, traitors, headstrong, haughty, lovers of pleasure rather than lovers of God, having a form of godliness but denying its power. And from such people turn away!"* (2 Timothy 3:1-5 NKJV).

If you continue to do your own thing and stubbornly refuse to walk in righteousness, the day will come when you won't know where to turn for help. Many will be deceived and no longer able to discern between truth and lies. They will be, *"Ever learning, and never able to come to the knowledge of the truth. Now as Jannes and Jambres withstood Moses, so do these also resist the truth: men of corrupt minds, reprobate concerning the faith. But they shall proceed no further"* (2 Timothy 3:7-9 NKJV).

The time is short. That is why I made a decision to daily climb my mountain and always keep my heart teachable and hungry for righteousness. I refuse to put it off. Daily I choose to surrender everything to God. I prepare my heart to keep it pure before God.

## Hang on to Truth by Cutting the Rope of Pleasing People

If I feel like I am at the end of my rope in a situation, I firmly hold on to the truth, which keeps me free from being a man pleaser. I cut that rope of pleasing people. I remind myself that the only thing that matters is pleasing God. Furthermore, my God-given position of righteousness guarantees that I am already pleasing to God because of Jesus. That is how I hang on and keep climbing.

We are living in the end times. Many churches are filled with compromise, trying to please people. They are walking in deception.

There is always a leader who will do what the people want, as opposed to what God wants. If you want a leader who will give you what you want, rather than what God wants, there will always be an Aaron available.

There will always be a leader who will do what the people want because he is not praying, worshipping, and plugging into God's Word. This type of leader spends more time before the people's face than God's. Therefore he spends his life pleasing people rather than living unto the Lord.

On the mountain, Moses heard from God. However, Aaron did not obey God; he was down in the valley listening to people. The Bible says, *"And Aaron said to them, 'Break off the golden earrings which are in the ears of your wives, your sons, and your daughters, and bring them to me.' So all the people broke off the golden earrings which were in their ears, and brought them to Aaron. And he received the gold from their hand, and he fashioned it with an engraving tool, and made a molded calf. Then they said, 'This is your god, O Israel, that brought you out of the land of Egypt!'"* (Exodus 32:2-4 NKJV).

There have been many times when I have met with people and God has shown me things about them. It isn't always easy when I have to tell them what He showed me. Sometimes He has me confront sin in their lives. If I worry about what they will think of me, I might not share what the Lord has said. But I am more concerned with being obedient to God than tickling man's ears.

I know that if God shows me something, it is because He wants to reach somebody. They may get mad at me, but eventually they will realize that I love them and I'm only obeying what God told me to do. We have to be more concerned with pleasing the Lord than pleasing people.

# Don't Hang on to Your Own Thing

We can't reach the top by doing our own thing. If we insist on doing our own thing, Jesus can't be Lord of our lives. Any time we choose our own way, our own ideas, our own goals or anything besides God, we are exalting that thing in our lives and making it into an idol. Even if it's a good thing, if we try to do it in our own ability as we think it should be done, then we are saying that we know better than God.

The children of Israel did their own thing; they made a golden calf and claimed that it was the god that brought them out of Egypt. They got tired of waiting for God and having someone else tell them what to do, so they decided to do things their own way.

I am talking about a people who had been in slavery for over 400 years. They saw God send plagues and deliver them out of Egypt. When they left, they saw God take the wealth of the world and put it in their hands. They saw God as a pillar of fire by night and a pillar of cloud by day. Not only that, but they also saw God split the Red Sea so they could walk across on dry ground.

How many times has God split the Red Sea for you? I can testify that, many times, God has made a way for me. The Israelites made a silly golden calf and claimed it had delivered them. If we don't climb

God's mountain, we make our own golden calf. It may be money, people, or things, but it is always something that won't matter eternally.

## Hang on to Forgiveness

When I felt like I was at the end of my rope with people who were mad at me, I hung on by forgiving them. Moses forgave people who were angry with him. He interceded in prayer for them. Moses loved people. He had to love them. He showed his passion for people when he stood before God and said, "Lord, change Your plan and Your thinking and relent from the fierceness of Your wrath!"

Moses wanted to see the Israelites receive God's best, but they were mad at him and were continually griping and complaining. There were times when Moses wanted them killed. He was upset, but God said, "Moses, it's okay. We will make it through this together."

It's a good thing that God and Moses never got into an agreement about the wrath thing. God would have said, "I am going to consume these people," and it would have been all over if Moses had simply said, "Go ahead."

People get upset if they can't have their way. But God loves them regardless, and we need to as well. God has given me a love for people so no matter what happens, I choose to forgive them with God's love.

When we love people, we hate to see them struggling and falling short of God's best for their lives. We hate to see them settle for anything less. We don't want them to be stuck in their circumstances and situations. It bothers us when we see them in debt and know that God wants them to prosper. It hurts us when we see them sick and know that God wants them well. It upsets us when we see them down and we know that God wants them up. It frustrates us when we see them compromising the promises of God.

We want to see these people we love on the mountaintop, but they have to make the choice to get there. We can only help them to let go of doing it their own way. They have to learn to walk in forgiveness and not hold on to offense or pain. Unless we let go of all these things, we will never be able to climb our mountain.

## Hang on to Encouragement

When we are at the end of our rope, we need people around us who will encourage us to hang on. There will always be people in our lives whom we are called to encourage, as well as people who are called to encourage us. When we are in the middle of a problem or a circumstance, we need the kind of people around us that will build us up rather than remind us of the problems we are facing.

When I was fighting for my life, I couldn't have anyone around me who wasn't speaking victory or faith. I have friends and family who are good, godly people, but they don't know how to believe or speak right. They weren't necessarily speaking blatantly wrong things, but they had a "bless your heart" attitude. If I had given in to that, I would have started to feel sorry for myself, and it would have cost me my life.

When we are fighting to hang on, we need to surround ourselves with people who will build us up and speak faith to us. We can't allow ourselves to wallow around in self-pity with a "poor me" attitude, or we could die. Anything that isn't building us up is keeping us in the same situation that we are already in.

It's like quicksand; if you are stuck in quicksand, it will eventually swallow you if you don't have someone pull you out. You will sink even if you don't move at all. Unless you are moving in a forward and upward motion, you will sink down. We need people who will throw us the lifeline of faith to help pull us out of the quicksand of self-pity.

When you are going through something, don't talk about it with everyone. You can talk to a few people who know how to pray and believe, but you need to ensure that you only surround yourself with people who will speak faith to you and not allow you to get into self-pity. You need people who will be bold to claim the promises of God for you when you feel your hope and faith start to wear thin.

Those who hang around my dad, my ministry leaders and me, are all family. We are all going to the top. We are going to pull others up to the top. I don't let Bible College students die and go to hell. I drag them out of defeat. I am not going to let the devil have them—period! I don't care how much they like me or dislike me; they can't hurt my feelings.

There is a promised land, a land of abundance, for you. Just stay focused and pursue all that you have been called to do. Hang on with diligence and keep climbing your mountain. There are people who will be impacted by your climb. Your destiny is bigger than just you. When your destiny is fully realized, it will change the lives of people around you.

# 5

# THE "STARTING OVER" PROCESS

*"If we confess our sins, he is faithful and just to forgive us our*
*sins, and to cleanse us from all unrighteousness."*

1 John 1:9

There were times I stumbled when climbing the mountain of the Lord, but I got up, dusted myself off, and got back on track. There are times when we all miss it or make mistakes, but the only way we can fail is if we don't get back up. I hung on by starting over. I'm alive and healthy today because of second chance miracles.

## Hang on by Testifying About Your Second Chance

There were many times when I felt like I had come to the end of my rope and had to start over. Many people don't realize that they can start over, but there is a starting over process. They seem to think that they have made too many mistakes or messed up too badly for God to use them, but our God is a Redeemer and He wants to redeem our mistakes and turn them into testimonies. The blood of Jesus can cleanse us, and the grace of God can restore us. Jesus loves us and has great plans for our lives. All we have to do is come to Him.

Many years ago, I had backslidden and turned my back on God. I had been through so much and seen so many hypocritical people that I didn't want any part of this so-called Christianity. I didn't sleep around or do anything like that; I just wanted to have a good time. I liked to go out to the clubs and dance; sometimes I would drink or do drugs.

I would taunt my dad by saying, "Does it bother you that you go out to all of these schools and get all these young people saved, and yet you can't even save your own daughter?" He had many well-known ministers come in and try to reach me, but I was too hard-hearted to change.

At one time, I pointed my finger at God and cried out, "I'll never serve You another day in my life! You took my mother away from me. You took Bobby away from me. I'll never serve You another day!" I made it a point, and for three and a half years, I didn't set foot in the door of a church. I had made my mind up.

Then God gave my dad a word through Brother and Sister Goodwin. They said, "Zona has gone too far. She will never come back on her own. When she comes in at night, you tell her that you love her and that God loves her, then don't say anything else because she doesn't believe anyone loves her."

So that's exactly what my dad did. For six months, I would come home in the middle of the night and he would call out to me. I would be smart with him, but he didn't say anything except what God told him to say.

Then one night as I was getting ready to go out with my friends, I told my dad that I didn't really want to go out with them. My dad jumped at the opportunity and asked me to stay at home with him, but just then my friends pulled up. My dad said, "What is God going to have to do to bring you back?"

I said, "He'll have to knock me in the head because I'm not going back."

After I left, my dad went in to the spare room, lay on the bed, and started praying. He said, "God, You heard what she said. Do whatever You have to do to bring her back to You." While I was at the club that night, I saw a vision of my dad's face in the corner of the club. It completely freaked me out, because I had always said that if I ever saw my dad in a club, I would never go back.

When I came home later, it was the middle of the night so I went to sleep in the spare room. I woke up a short while later and saw what appeared to be a person the size of two men, sitting beside my bed with his legs crossed. His belt buckle was eye level with me. He had long hair and was wearing a bright yellow shirt with a striped tie.

After I saw him, he stood up, walked out of the bedroom door, and went down the hall. I covered my head with a blanket and tiptoed down the hallway to see where he went. As soon as I peeked around the corner, I saw him waiting for me. When he saw me, he turned and walked through the back door like it wasn't there.

I ran down the hallway to my dad's bedroom and started banging on the door. I told him what I saw and he explained that it was my angel. That was the last time I ever went to the clubs. Many of the friends I used to run around with are now dead. I probably would be too if my dad hadn't stood in the gap and did what was necessary to reach me. God doesn't want anyone to die and go to hell, but He will never force anyone to serve Him.

After I repented, I got back on track and began climbing my mountain. I read and studied God's Word, prayed, worshipped God, and got into His presence. Then, I followed His voice and became free to do His plan for my life. I made up my mind to step over to a life of full surrender, to give my heart to Jesus, and live like nothing else mattered but Him.

There is no room for "big" sermons. I tell the Bible College students, "Don't add to sermons. Don't exaggerate. That is lying. Just tell it like it is. If you ever fail, just tell them like it is. Tell them how you got up, dusted yourself off, and started all over."

## Hang on to Your Second Chance Miracles

I encourage myself by remembering my second chance miracles. I do this by sharing my testimony without shame. I just tell what God has done in my life. God has given me many miracles, which gave me a second chance to climb God's mountain.

The devil tried to kill me when I was a baby. I was born premature and only weighed three pounds, ten ounces. My dad said he could hold me in one hand. I was so small that they couldn't even feed me with a bottle; they had to use an eye dropper and feed me a drop at a time. At that time, my family was Baptist and knew nothing about standing in faith or believing for miracles, but God still kept me.

From ages two through four, I kept getting sick. I would have very high fevers, even to the extent that they would have to put me in a tub of ice to try and make my temperature go back down. I was rushed to Johns Hopkins Hospital, where they diagnosed me as having influenza of the blood stream. They were able to help me, but I was stuck in the hospital for a month living in a quarantine tent. My dad had limited visitation and wasn't able to hold me at all. But once again, God saved my life.

Another time when I was five, I was playing by the road near our house. A car drove by and somehow I got pulled underneath. The driver had no idea that I was caught under his car, so he dragged me up the street a ways before the car dropped me. My dad was terrified, but God protected me and I was fine. The only scar I had was on my knee.

The devil continued to attack me, and I began to sleepwalk. One night my dad and mom woke up and couldn't find me anywhere. The neighbor called them and told them I was asleep on their couch. I could have ended up anywhere, but God's angels protected me.

After God visited my dad and called him to serve Him, things changed drastically in my life. My parents got divorced and I went to live with my dad in Cleveland, Tennessee. He met a man named Brother Littlefield, who greatly influenced him and got him involved with the Full Gospel Business Men's Fellowship (where he met Kenneth Hagin Sr. and Lester Sumrall).

I got saved and filled with the Spirit, and my dad learned how to walk in faith. Through his faith and confession, the growths on my body left. When I backslid, he stood in the gap for me and I came back to God. Many of the friends I was partying with died at young ages, but God protected me—even when I wasn't serving Him.

The Lord delivered me from low potassium. This may not seem like a big deal, but remember the heart is a muscle, so with potassium as low as what I was experiencing, I would have died if God had not been with me. Another time, the doctors didn't know what was wrong with me and diagnosed me as having lupus. They said I had thirty days to live and told me to get my affairs in order. But once again, God stepped in and healed me.

When my daughter was young, I was bitten by a black widow spider. As they were loading me into the ambulance to take me to the hospital, I saw my angel for the second time. He climbed into the ambulance with me and told me not to be afraid. He said that I was going to be alright.

Through all of these attacks, God protected me. However, these miracles came through the faith of my father. There came a time when I had to use my own faith to get my miracle. In 1994, God sent me a friend of our family's named Doc Horton. He was a medical doctor and God told me to have him check me out. It was then that I discovered I had swollen parathyroid glands, which caused calcium deposits in my kidneys thereby producing kidney failure. So I had a parathyroidectomy and was placed on dialysis.

I didn't want to be on dialysis. I wanted an instant miracle like my dad had gotten for me before, but God used dialysis to meet me where my faith was. In this, He prolonged my life. Too many people put God in a box and try to tell Him how they want their miracle, but all they are doing is tying God's hands. We need to let Him do what He needs to do in order to meet us where our faith is. God can use doctors and medicine the same way He can use supernatural miracles.

After I was first diagnosed, I completely backed off of ministry. I felt like a hypocrite and a fraud. I thought, *How can I be on life-support and teach faith?* But God got hold of my dad and he came bursting into my office, saying, "Your miracle is in your teaching and preaching! What are you going to do about it?"

I said, "I guess I'm going to teach and preach."

Then my dad told my assistant to start booking my meetings. I had to schedule my ministry trips around dialysis sessions. During this time, the devil kept trying to get me to quit or back off, but I refused!

At one point, I tried to be super-spiritual and took myself off of dialysis. I looked like I was full of faith but in the natural, I was dying. Eventually I called a well-known kidney doctor and told him who I was and what I had done. He said that he would meet me in the emergency room, because he wanted to meet anyone who was stubborn enough to be off of dialysis for twenty-one days and live to tell about it!

The doctor put me back on dialysis and they only took nine pounds of fluid off of me, which was a miracle. The doctor told me that he knew I had someone watching over me…and I did. God had protected me, despite my stupid attempt to "show-off" how full of faith I was.

I had my first kidney transplant in the spring of 1996. Unfortunately, my body rejected the kidney and I had to go back on dialysis. I was on dialysis for a total of two years and ten months. I did everything the doctor told me, down to the letter. I was doing everything I knew to do in the natural and the spiritual to get a miracle, but I was still dying.

One day, I was getting dressed and walked past a mirror. I honestly saw what I really looked like for the first time; I weighed sixty-nine pounds and looked like skin and bones. I threw myself on the bed and cried out to God, "God, whatever You have to do to save my life, I ask You to do it!"

The next week, I received a call saying that they had found a kidney for me. God met me where my faith was and I lived. I maintained a normal, healthy life for many years before the devil tried to take me out again.

The next incident happened when I was driving to work with my daughter. Two young girls cut us off and our car went into a ditch. I had to be cut out of the car. If my daughter, Lee, had not thrown herself in front of me, the air bag could have killed me. But instead, I walked away with a broken collar bone. As I was worshiping God that following week, He supernaturally came into my living room and healed my collar bone!

The devil is crazy and has continually tried to kill me. He has tried to put congestive heart failure, CRV virus, and more kidney failure on me. But I keep pressing on, doing what God has called me to do, walking in faith, and worshipping God. I turn every attack into a testimony and an opportunity to share the love of God. Even when I was fighting for my life in the hospital, I witnessed to everyone who came into my room. I make up my mind every day to stay strong and walk in faith.

God is a God of second chances. I can't imagine my life without Him. Jesus has given me so many miracles that it would take many books to tell of all the great things He has done. Keep sharing the things Jesus did for you. Keep winning souls. Keep hanging on. Climb the mountain. No matter what happens, never quit!

I made the decision to continue climbing the mountain of the Lord, going from glory to glory. Even if you have started over, continue forward and make that climb up your mountain.

# 6

# HANG OUT WITH RIGHT RELATIONSHIPS

*"Greater love hath no man than this,*
*that a man lay down his life for his friends."*

John 15:13

I hang out with the right people. When I feel I'm at the end of my rope, I can keep climbing to the top by tying in to the right relationships. If we aren't tied in to the right people, we can easily slip and fall into the valley of fear and hopelessness.

Choose Heaven; cut off all of the ungodly relationships that will take you through hell. We will never fulfill God's purpose unless we are connected with godly relationships. Light can't mix with darkness. Ungodly relationships darken our hearts, causing us to be spiritually blind and deaf.

If we love God but get involved with people who are in darkness, those people will turn our hearts away from God. Then our hearts will become hard and filled with darkness. To keep our hearts soft and pliable, we need to get into God's presence. The Holy Spirit guides us into all truth, causing us to hate sin and love righteousness. To see God's glory, the real expression of His will and plan for our lives, we must continually move forward.

I love all people, but God has given me a special love for young people. God desires to use the pure in heart. God is looking for those whose hearts seek His love, His Word, and His presence. He will do great and mighty things with the young people who are totally sold out to Him. That is why we have to teach this generation to stay tied in to the right people.

Whether we are young or old, God is telling us to get up so He can show Himself strong in our lives. Run after God's glory with all your heart. Worship Him. Mean business with God. He will show Himself strong and do great things in and through you when you seek Him with a pure heart (2 Chronicles 16:9).

## Hang with People Who Support You

I wouldn't be able make it to the top if I didn't hang with people who support me. To make it to the top, tie in to the right people. The number one lesson required for us to complete a major climb is that we can't make it to the top by ourselves. This is also true in our spiritual lives. We can't do it alone; it is nearly impossible.

Have you ever seen or read a story about the people who climb Mount Everest or Mount Kilimanjaro? When people want to climb these mountains, they know they need a strong team. If they tried to do it by themselves, they could get hurt, lost or even die. They start out hiking in a group and when it gets to a certain point, they have to tie themselves together with a strong rope. They hook their harness onto a long lead rope until they are all connected. Then they continue up the mountain. They do this because it helps to keep everyone together, and if someone is in trouble, everyone is signaled immediately. If a team member fell, they could use the rope to find him and pull him to safety.

This is also true in our lives. We need to have people we are accountable to who can speak into our lives. They will know what's going on in our life so if they see potential trouble, they can be there to help steady us. If we start to get off-track, they can help get us going in the right direction again. That is why we are the Body of Christ. We work and function together as a body.

We watch out for one another. The devil would love to make us panic and feel like we are alone in our struggle, but if we stay roped together with godly people, we will never stray far from what God has for us. Together, we will be able to climb the mountain.

## Hang on to Your Anchor

When we climb a mountain, if we get into a mess and stumble, we need to stop climbing and anchor ourselves. If we don't, we will fall and die. If we are climbing a glacier or mountain that is permanently covered in snow and ice, we need to use an ice axe. An ice axe is used to save our lives (or the life of a teammate) if we start to slide. We must strike it into the ice, then it will keep us from falling further.

I have been trained that if you are facing a situation in your life, you should find a Scripture that covers your case and stand on it. When Betty Baxter's mother believed for her daughter's miracle, she held on to Mark 9:23, which says that all things are possible to him that believes. She clung to this verse as her anchor for fourteen years before Betty was made whole.

When I was standing for the miracle for my kidneys, I held on to the parable of the woman with the unjust judge and the story of the woman with the issue of blood. I cried out to Jesus to avenge me of kidney failure and visualized myself touching the hem of His garment. At that moment when hope was fading, I focused on these verses and hung on to the promise of God. These biblical accounts helped me stay anchored while I went through dialysis and fought for my life.

If we want to receive our miracle, we can't allow fearful thoughts to distract us from our climb. When fearful thoughts come, immediately stop what you're doing and worship God—submit to Him. When the devil comes, we need to make sure we are equipped with the sword of the Spirit. We must hook that powerful anchor to the side of the mountain and say, "Wait a minute devil, I'm not falling down! I'm not quitting! I'm going on! Satan, you're a liar! Take your hands off of me and my family in Jesus' name!" God's Word is our anchor.

## Hanging with Right Relationships Will Keep You from Falling

We don't come to church just to sing songs and go through services. We come to church to build relationships. Some people say, "It does not matter if I go to church or not; I'll just get the CD or podcast." To this I respond, "When we go to Heaven, we'll send you a video."

Life as a Christian is not about getting ministry material or listening to different preachers; it is about relationships. We are called to be the Body of Christ. We need to work together and get to know one another. We need to get involved in a local church and meet the pastor and people there, getting to know them and letting them get to know us. We need to get next to each other, take hands, worship God together, have lunch together, and share with each other.

Building relationships is what it is all about. When we attend church or Bible College, we can build relationships that will last for the rest of our lives. To build relationships, we need to spend time with people and fellowship with them. When we fall into a crevice of life without a rope, we will wish that we had built better relationships.

There is a good reason that God said it isn't good for man to be alone. This doesn't just apply to being married. Too many Christians get flaky because they don't want to commit to a local church and pastor. They think they can get everything that they need from watching preachers on TV or listening to teaching series. They say that they are accountable to God alone. But there are things that we can gain from being connected with a local church that we can't get on our own.

We need to be accountable to people, because it is too easy to justify our actions or tune out the voice of God when we are doing something we know we are not supposed to be doing. A true accountability partner will stop us and make us see the danger that we are walking toward. A local church body can be there to support us through difficult times, not to mention the people who could benefit from us being involved in their life as well.

## Hang with the Right Spouse

When God sends the right spouse to you, he or she will pull you up the mountain, rather than work against you. When you are busy working for the Lord, God knows what you need and will send the right person into your life. That happened to me after my first husband died. God blessed me with the sweetest, most wonderful husband in the world.

I hadn't planned on getting remarried and made my mind up that I was going to remain single and just serve God. I had several men who were calling and wanted to date me, but I didn't want to go out with any of them.

Then one day, a man by the name of Terry Morrow called me. This was significant, because when I was divorced from Bobby for three years, I dated Terry. I dated him for several months while I remained single but eventually I broke it off, remarried Bobby, and never looked back.

I didn't see Terry again until three days before Bobby died. We ran into him at a restaurant on a Sunday afternoon, and he and Bobby made peace with each other. That night Bobby had an aneurism and went into a coma. He died the following Wednesday morning.

Several months later, I was talking to a friend about the situation and said, "I'll tell you one thing, if Terry Morrow is single, he'll call me, but that is the devil if I ever knew it." I didn't want to talk to him because I didn't think I was going to date anyone. Sometimes, you can get your mind fixed one way and not make room for the will of God.

One day, I came into the office and there was a message for me: "Ms. Zona, a man named Terry Morrow called. Please call back." I took the message to a friend and I said, "This is demonic. Look at this. This is a snake if I ever saw it. I bind you, devil!" Still, I had my mind set on thinking this was not God; I was determined not to date anybody.

The next week, Terry and I talked. We continued to talk on the telephone off and on for a month. During this time, I still didn't want to date anybody, so we just met in restaurants occasionally. Then, we began to see each other in a group setting.

To make a long story short, we ended up getting married. I never let Terry come to my house to pick me up until two months before we got married. He was only allowed to come to my door to pick me up and drop me off. It was a pure relationship.

My first husband, Bobby was a very faithful husband and a good Bible teacher. I am very grateful for my time with him. But, I am also very thankful to God for bringing me Terry at just the right time. He is such a humble and gentle man and has been such a blessing to my life. Today, our marriage is fun and we have a ball. Terry makes me laugh. He is such a joy to be around. He isn't high pressure or high maintenance and he never complains. He loves the church and the people. He has been the icing on my cake.

Being in a godly marriage helps us stay strong in our relationship with the Lord. We are tied together and strengthen each other. We stand with each other through trials and build up each other's faith when one of us is under attack. Terry may not be in full-time ministry, but God sent him to me and he is a blessing in my life!

# Hang with People
# of Like Vision in God's Will

I feel support when I feel I am coming to the end of my rope when I hang with people who are of like vision. Right relationships won't let us go. They pull us out of the ditch. But we can't climb together if we don't share a vision.

While on a mountain, if one person is moving slowly, everybody else will slow down. This is because the rope maintains the distance between the climbers. If one person starts moving fast, the others will all start moving at the same pace.

Likewise, with the right people, I can pace my life. I never live a double standard. People are watching us and will follow our example. We can make the difference between a person going to Heaven or hell. Our godly influence and pure heart can make the difference between them loving or rejecting Christ. When we tie in to wise people, they will help us get into God's divine will for our lives.

# Hanging with Right Relationships
# Will Help Save Your Life

When I feel I'm at the end of my rope, right relationships save my life. If we face a bad report or life threatening situation, it is extremely important for us to only tie in to relationships marked by strong faith.

If I had hung with people who felt sorry for me, wouldn't get firm with me, or wouldn't teach me how to walk by faith when I was in a life threatening situation, I would have died. In the same way, we need to get around godly men and women who are filled with faith and can pull us out of despair.

Whenever I face a life threatening situation, I listen to God's Word as I stand alongside strong men and women of faith. I refuse to tie in to people who will let me talk defeat. I hang around those who will encourage me and help lift me higher. They are strong in the Lord and the power of His might (Ephesians 6:10).

To illustrate this, let me backtrack to a special day when my late husband, Bobby, spiritually pulled me up the mountain by teaching me how to stand firm. He taught me how to talk and act in faith rather than fear. It helped save my life.

One day I went home and said, "I'm tired, Bobby." He said, "Don't say that! You're not tired! Don't ever say that again, Zona!"

I started crying. He said, "Stop crying! You're not weak! You're strong! You are not tired!"

When he said that, I stopped talking defeat and got rid of that negative attitude. I didn't have anybody cut me slack for anything. Instead, I surrounded myself with people who encouraged me to walk in strength and see the victory of God in my life.

I praise God for the right relationships I had. When I got tired, they were continuously strong. If I got weary, they lifted me up. They tied in to me and held on to the rope. When I was about to fall, they dug in with their faith and held on. I might have been dangling, but they were strong and solid.

I have developed relationships with people who carry the same vision I have, who will help fulfill that vision. We have tied in to right relationships through our church board. These board members have the same vision we have and, no matter what, our ministry will stay above reproach.

Before you tie in to a spiritual leader, you need to know if they have the fruit of a genuine worshipper. You need to know if they put God's Word first in their life. Tie in to a pastor who won't compromise to sin—one to whom Jesus means everything. The Bible says to test the spirits before you develop relationships with people (1 John 4:1). We must only tie in to people who are proven to have godly character in order to avoid adversity in our lives.

Develop relationships with people who will help you move forward in your destiny. If you delight yourself in the Lord, He will give you the desires of your heart concerning relationships (Psalm 37:4). That is exactly what God will do if you worship Him with a pure heart; He will put the right relationships in your path—relationships that will tie in with you and keep you out of destruction!

# 7

# CUT ROPES OF WRONG RELATIONSHIPS

*"He who walks with wise men will be wise,*
*but the companion of fools will be destroyed."*

Proverbs 13:20 NKJV

We can't reach the top of our mountain if we are tied in with the wrong people. We have to discern wrong relationships and cut our ties with them. We need to connect with people who will bring us up, instead of those who will bring us down. That is the only way to accomplish God's will for our lives.

## Don't Hang with Foolish People

We need to examine the people we are hanging around. We need to build relationships with wise men and women who have the type of relationship with God that we want. If we partner with people who know God as well as we do or better, they will keep us moving forward and getting stronger.

Hanging with a complainer, gossiper, or negative person is dangerous. They will bring us down and destroy us. Foolish people never lift us up into the things of God or help us focus on eternity. Instead, they pull us down into destruction and hell. They hinder us from fulfilling our divine destiny.

As the saying goes, *you become like those you hang out with*. If we always hang out with people who are foolish, whose only priority is having a good time, then we will begin to think and act the same way. This will cause us to lose focus on fulfilling God's will for our lives. If we hang out with people who want more of God in their lives and strive to live like Christ, we will do the same. We need to find people who will make us want to be better, do more, and try harder, as opposed to people who will stunt our spiritual growth.

If we foster relationships with fools, we will become like them and be destroyed. We need to cut the connections with these types of people so they don't drag us down. If we allow them to drag us down, it will not only harm us, it will also affect our families and those connected with us. We can pray, love, and witness to them, but we can't allow their choices to cause us to stumble.

With this dynamic in mind, how many people are you dragging down because you won't cut ties with negative relationships? Are you willing to risk those who are closest to you because you're still trying to hold on to someone who is bringing you down? Anyone who isn't helping you move forward is holding you back. You have to make a decision to cut that tie. Like 1 Corinthians 15:33 says, "Bad company corrupts good character" (NIV).

If you continue to hold on to these types of relationships, you will find yourself tainted by the lifestyle of unbelief. Light doesn't mix with darkness. Don't compromise because it can cost both your life and the lives of those around you.

We can't continue to stay roped up with people who hold us back from following God. This truth is where the rubber meets the road. Are you willing to sacrifice your life, marriage, future, kids, money, peace of mind, or relationship with God for a relationship with someone who doesn't even care about the will of God? You need to follow God regardless of who comes with you. Love and pray for others, but don't allow natural relationships to cost you your relationship with God.

## Hang with People Who Are Going Where You Are Going

I can't have relationships with people who aren't in unity with me. I choose to only walk with people who are going to help me reach my destination. If a couple wanted to take a vacation together but one person wanted to go skiing while the other wanted to go to the beach, there would be no unity there. Neither of these things are bad, but in order to have fellowship, a couple has to agree together.

The same thing is true in our lives and ministries. There is no unity if one person goes this way and the other goes that way. Neither person may be doing anything wrong, but their paths are headed in different directions. To be in ministry together, we must have the same goal and purpose. We have to be going in the same direction.

This is also true regarding fellowship with people who don't believe the same way you do. You have to worship and serve the same God as those you hang out with. If you have friends whose priority in life is their money, image, or career, it is going to be very hard for the two of you to be joined together.

I'm better equipped to reach my destiny because of those who have gone before me. They did it by themselves and in doing so, they have left a standard for me to follow. They are living examples of the Word of God, which they teach and preach. I refuse to listen to the instruction of people who haven't proven to live godly lives. If we follow those who aren't godly examples, the blind will be leading the blind and we will both fall into the ditch.

## Cut the Ropes
## of Approval Seeking

Don't let the devil take you out with feelings of rejection brought on by the desire for man's approval. When I was young, I did everything I could to make my dad proud of me. I would trace a picture of a horse and take it to him, pretending that I had drawn it free-hand. He would praise me and tell me how good it was.

This went on for several months before my dad finally caught on. One day he said to me, "Draw the horse in front of me." I was nervous but I agreed to do it because I knew it would make him happy. Well, that horse ended up looking like it was deformed and I got a spanking for lying and trying to deceive my dad. I never did that again!

I loved my dad so much (and still do), but he traveled a lot when I was a child. I continually tried to find ways to make him stay with me. One time, I even pretended to be sick to the point where I ended up in the hospital, just so my dad wouldn't leave. He was my world, and I was consumed with being with him and making him proud of me.

I believe that many of us are like that; we will do anything to please other people. We base our self-worth on whether or not other people like us or on what they think about us. We want people to stay around us, so we do whatever it takes to keep them close.

I desperately wanted my dad's approval and stayed that way until my daughter was born. It was then that I began to understand unconditional love. I knew that there was nothing my daughter could ever do to make me love her more, nor was there anything she could do that would make me stop loving her. I love her for who she is, not for what she can do. God feels the same way about us. He loves us simply because we are His children, not because He wants something from us. Discovering what unconditional love meant set me free in many areas of my life. This all happened many years ago, but I'm still walking free from that bondage.

To stay on the right track, we need to prepare ourselves with a strong foundation of God's Word. We need to cultivate right relationships that will pull us up into God's will. We never know what will happen in our future, so we need to be prepared with the Word of God.

If I didn't have the Word of God, I wouldn't have made it when my kidneys were attacked. I felt so humiliated while I was on the dialysis machine. It seemed as though all of my dignity was thrown out the window each time I sat there with those needles sticking in my arm. Then afterwards, I would have to go back to church and speak on faith.

I felt like a hypocrite because, while I was the daughter of a general of faith, I still had to sit on life-support several times a week.

Thankfully, I had right relationships. That's important when we are going through great adversity. When I was too tired to stand on my own, I had good people who would stand with me and lift my arms. They didn't care what things looked like because they had faith that I would make it through.

My faith isn't built up when I'm around people who don't know the Word. When you are full of God's Word, it won't work to be around people who don't live the Word. Jesus' sheep follow Him because they know His voice (John 10:27). Sheep are trained to hear and follow the voice of their shepherd—His voice alone (John 10:3-4). If a stranger talks to the sheep, they won't follow his voice because the only voice they know is that of their shepherd. Sheep run from the voice of a stranger. If you are around other people who love God's Word, you won't follow strange voices (John 10:5).

## Hang with Jesus as the Center of Your Life

Jesus is the most important person in my life; I give Him first place and depend on Him completely. In the natural, the people we are presently serving and depending on won't be there forever. That's why I make Jesus the center of my life as I establish right relationships.

People are transitional in life. There is a saying that people are in your life for a reason, a season, or for life. This means that some people are in our lives to either help us through something, help us learn something, or will always be connected with us.

We have to learn who these people are in our life in order to properly relate to them. If we are consumed with trying to please people and keep them in our lives, we won't be able to focus on pleasing the One who really matters—Jesus. He is the only constant in our lives. Besides, we will never be able to please everyone all the time. There will always be those who are dissatisfied with what we do. Actually, we can kill ourselves trying to be a man pleaser, when we should be living to be a God-pleaser.

Make Jesus the center of your life by tying in to the Holy Ghost. He has to be the only thing that matters in your life. You have to make the choice to stay filled with the Spirit. Regardless of what happens in life, you can't allow yourself to become distracted because that will stop you from fulfilling your destiny. Let your thirst for God be greater than anything else on earth. Desire to stay filled with His presence and you'll begin to crave the things of God.

Whatever we hunger for is what will control our lives. If we are thirsty for the things of the world and the pleasures of sin, those desires will control us. God's wants to be our desire. He wants us to hunger and thirst after Him. When we pursue Him, we make Jesus the center of our life. In Matthew 6:25-33, Jesus promised that when we seek Him first and make His kingdom top priority in our lives, He will add all other things unto us. When we make God our priority, we are positioning ourselves to receive everything He has for us.

## Don't Hang with People Who Drag You Down into Crevices

Wrong relationships will drag us down into crevices. I have personally seen people drug down into the crevices of life. They got out of God's will because they were tied to wrong relationships. Several have lost ministries, businesses, and families. I'm passionate about helping people avoid this because it is such a terrible thing.

Choose to be grounded and rooted in the Word and trained by the Holy Ghost. Get away from all bad relationships. Cut the ties or else you will work yourself to death. I've seen so many people slide down into crevices of divorce, drugs, alcohol, sin, and despair.

Over the years, we've seen many Bible College students get distracted by wrong relationships and leave school before they were ready. There was one young man in particular who attended our Bible College and was on fire for God, but he left and got involved with some people he shouldn't have. Ultimately, he became overcome with the love of money.

Later, I saw one of his family members at a convention and asked where he was. She responded that he hadn't come to the meeting. Then I asked if he was serving the Lord and she said he wasn't. She gave me his phone number so I decided to call him. When I got hold of him, I said, "It doesn't matter how much money you are making. I don't care what you're doing. You were on fire for the Lord. If you don't stop chasing money and get yourself rooted and grounded in the Word, then you are going to end up right back where you started."

He didn't see the big picture, so I had to warn him about the dangers of the path he was on. He had attended Bible College and was trained in the Word of God, but he allowed himself to get tied in with the wrong people and they drug him down the wrong path. There is nothing wrong with working a job or making money, but if God has called us to do something else, then we can't afford to go another direction.

Just because a path isn't bad or sinful doesn't mean that it isn't the wrong path for us to be on. And when we are not being obedient to God, we are opening ourselves up to the attacks of the devil.

Never yoke yourself with unbelievers. They will drag you down. Light does not mix with darkness (2 Corinthians 6:14). Take note of the people who have stopped climbing up the mountain. They no longer take time to read their Bible or pray. They don't live what they profess. They make excuses so they don't have to be faithful in church.

The devil will do whatever he can to destroy our lives. Whatever works of hell we will put up, those are the works we will have in our lives. We need to connect with people who will help us stay built up and strong. They will speak the truth to us and stop us from going down the wrong path. Not everyone can be that kind of friend, so we need to be careful who we hang around with.

## Don't Hang with Abusive Relationships

Don't tie on to abusive relationships filled with constant drama. Abusive words can crush your will and destroy you. My mother told me, "You're the reason your father and I are getting a divorce. If you had not been born, I would have had your daddy all to myself and we wouldn't be getting a divorce." She said this to make me feel her pain.

I dreaded going clothes shopping with my mother because she always talked about how fat I was. Whenever she took me shopping, I would hide under the clothes rack. She would say, "I guess we need to go to the chubby sizes." I would get so embarrassed, I would hide. She couldn't find me and I wouldn't come out.

I hated the word "fat." I hated people squeezing my cheeks and saying, "Oh, you are so cute." I allowed the devil's thoughts to be formed in my mind, telling me that I wasn't cute because I was constantly harped on about my weight. When I got older, I didn't like myself. I didn't like the way I looked. I didn't like the way I felt. I thought I was too fat. I allowed negative words to mold how I viewed myself. If we are not careful to use kind words, we can ruin a person's self-image.

Abusive relationships will destroy us, while right relationships will encourage us and help us succeed in life. There are many examples of right relationships in the Bible. Many times in Scripture, we see how individuals assisted each other: Jonathan and David; Naomi and Ruth; Esther and Mordecai; Paul and Timothy; Jesus and John. These individuals lifted each other up.

I have many strong relationships with godly men and women in my life. I can go to these people when I have a need and they will stand with me and help build my faith. When trials come, if we are tied together, we can help each other stay strong and encouraged. We need to be connected with people who believe in us.

# Don't Hang with Devils!

Many people are easily deceived and seduced by doctrines of devils, thinking they are hearing from God. We will depart from the faith if we hang with deceiving, seductive spirits; *"Now the Spirit speaketh expressly, that in the latter times some shall depart from the faith, giving heed to seducing spirits, and doctrines of devils"* (1 Timothy 4:1).

These people attend church and hear the Word taught, but when they go home they are occupied with other things. They don't know what the Bible says and are easily deceived. To keep from being deceived, we must do everything we can to get a strong foundation in God's Word. We must read and study the Bible, get right relationships, flow with the Spirit of God, and not tie on to devils.

Not only do we need to cut ties with bad relationships, but we also have to clearly discern familiar spirits. Once discerned, we must resist the devil and he will flee from us. As I stated before, the devil comes to kill, steal, and destroy. Nothing about the devil is good. He is a liar and the father of lies. He will tell us whatever he thinks might get us off track. He will try to make us feel bad about something good or good about something bad. He has been studying people for thousands of years and knows how to manipulate them. He will put us in situations that tempt us to go back to our old lifestyles.

Sometimes the devil will use music, sometimes people; just know that he will use whatever it takes to keep us emotionally and mentally distracted. If we aren't grounded in the Word, we might believe his lies and find ourselves stuck in a negative whirlpool.

## Hang on by Being Properly Equipped

Preparation means everything. Everyone wants to be successful, but success doesn't happen overnight. Every successful person has put in years of hard work to prepare themselves for where they are now. We have to put time and effort into learning the necessary skills and acquiring the proper equipment. If we try to climb a mountain without proper preparation, training, and equipment, it could cost us our lives.

In boxing, they say champions are made in the gym, not in the ring. Boxers know that if they want to become champions, they need to put in a lot of long hours training at the gym. They will spend months and years training before a big match. Likewise, if we want to succeed in our Christian walk, we need to prepare and learn how to use the tools that God has given us.

Part of proper preparation is having the right gear and knowing how to use it. To climb a mountain in icy snow, we need to have special spikes on our boots. To keep our footing, we need to be able to drive our boots down into the snow or ice.

In the Bible, Paul talks about putting on the full armor of God in order to stand against the tricks of the devil (Ephesians 6:11, 13-14). Then the Scripture says, *"And having shod your feet with the preparation of the gospel of peace"* (Ephesians 6:15 NKJV). This is an illustration of special boots the Roman soldiers would wear. The shoes had spikes on the bottom which made it easier for them to walk over rough terrain. If they didn't wear these boots, it would be a lot harder and take a lot longer for them to get where they needed to go.

Our spiritual feet must be shod with the preparation of the gospel of peace. Instead of being well shod with the preparation of the Gospel, most people are "slipshod." They aren't consistent in God's Word. They go to church once or twice a week, but they don't apply the Word because they aren't shod with the preparation of the gospel of peace. They aren't prepared to walk through the trial they are facing.

We need to be prepared to fight for our healing long before we are attacked with cancer. If we wait until we are attacked to stand on the Word, then we will be stuck playing catch-up to the devil. We have to know the Word ahead of time so when the attack comes, we will immediately be able to stand against it and stop it from taking root in our body, mind or spirit.

Tragically, many Christians are not properly prepared and when attacks come, they end up backsliding. Backslidden people don't want to come to church because they are embarrassed that they have slipped back into the world. They don't want to get around their Christian friends because they have messed up. They don't want others to find out that they have been doing some crazy stuff. Their pride and ego hold them away. They say, "I don't want to go around those Christians because they will judge me."

Although real Christians won't approve of sin, they won't judge you; they will help you. Genuine Christians will hold you up and stop you from sliding. The reason people slide is because they aren't well shod. You have to wear the right boots so you can dig into the mountain and keep from sliding.

You can't go to the top of your mountain by yourself. You must have right relationships. Your feet need to be shod with the Gospel. You have to hook up with successful people. Most importantly, you must be hooked up with God.

# 8

# MAKE YOUR LOAD LIGHTER

*"Therefore we also, since we are surrounded by so great a cloud of witnesses, let us lay aside every weight, and the sin which so easily ensnares us, and let us run with endurance the race that is set before us."*

Hebrews 12:1 NKJV

Before climbing to the top of the mountain, I had to lay aside every weight and distraction that hindered me from reaching my goal. After letting go of those things, I was able to run with endurance the race that was set before me. Allow me to exchange some terminology as we look at that verse again: *"… let us lay aside every weight, and the sin which so easily ensnares us, and let us <u>climb</u> with endurance the <u>mountain</u> that is set before us."*

We set every weight aside when we start worshipping the Lord. When athletes train for events, they use weights to help build up their muscles. They practice with them so their body can get used to the extra resistance. Then when it comes time to compete and they shed the weights, their bodies find the challenge easier because they had prepared for more. But in order for this strategy to work, they actually have to take the additional weights off before they race.

We can't win a race while carrying extra weights. These extra weights are for training purposes only. If we want to win, we have to take off the weights that will cause us to stumble, slow down, and ultimately lose. In order to go to the top, we have to let go of all distractions and focus solely on our goals.

Years ago when I had my fitness center, I used to sponsor marathons for various local charities. I had a friend who had multiple sclerosis, so I would sponsor benefits for charities like that. I noticed this about the various runners (especially the professionals) - they don't wear heavy clothing. Everything they have on is light and easy to move in. We need to be the same way when we face a challenge; we can't afford to carry any extra weight.

I attended certification clinics when I owned the fitness center in order to maintain my instructor's license. The clinics would begin on Friday and end on Sunday and consisted of various trials. I would be in excruciating pain by the end of the weekend because of all of the intense training we had to do.

I knew that I couldn't have any extra equipment with me during the trial sessions. I needed to carry only the required basics for my routine. If I had worn extra weights or had on too much clothing, I would have worn myself out before I could finish.

Going through those certification trials is like running a race or climbing a mountain. We only need to take what we need for the journey. We need to pack the essentials and let go of anything and everything that could slow us down or hold us back. Some things may be in our lives right now in order to train us for what is to come, but we can't let those things hold us back from ultimate success!

## Don't Take Things You Don't Need

There are many things that aren't needed when climbing mountains. When we climb the highest peaks, the less equipment we have to carry, the better off we are. If you have ever seen documentaries about the teams that climb the "extreme" peaks, you will notice that they leave some gear behind at each level. The higher they climb, the harder the climb becomes. They can't afford to carry any extra weight. It isn't that the extra equipment wouldn't be helpful; it just isn't necessary for survival and would hinder them from reaching their goal. Once the gear has served its purpose, it is set aside because it would hinder more than it would help. After reaching the summit, climbers can collect their extra equipment on their descent.

Mountain climbers need food when climbing. As long as they are in the lowlands, they can live on junk food (such as soda, chips, candy, and popcorn). However, when they want to climb a mountain, they need to eat wholesome foods. They have to watch their diet and train their bodies before they begin the climb. If they're planning to go higher, they will have to care about what goes into their bodies.

We need to be the same way in our Christian walk. If we want to climb higher and do something for God, we can't afford to feed our spirits "junk food." When we are serious about our walk with God, we will make sure that we are feasting on His Word and drinking in

His presence. We won't allow the petty things of the flesh to be our sustenance, but rather we will seek the Lord to fill our needs.

## Don't Hang on to Negative Emotions

I can't carry the weight of fear and still reach my destiny. Neither can you. When we are running a race to win, fear will try to attack us and thoughts of quitting will run through our minds.

At one point, the doctor had given me thirty days to live. I had been busy living my life and doing good works, but in the process, I had allowed myself to get distracted from the things of God. I wasn't as built up as I could have been. So when the devil brought this diagnosis, thoughts of quitting flooded my mind. A spirit of death tried to come on me, but I made it leave me in Jesus' name!

We have to resist the devil and trust in God. We have to keep our minds fixed on God, His Word and His promises. Then it doesn't matter what comes our way, we won't be afraid of evil reports because our hearts are fixed on Him.

With the last health attack that I faced, God had been preparing me for over a year in advance. He told me to read *How to Live and Not Die* every day until He told me to stop. He said this because He knew I would need it. I had no idea what was coming up, but I was obedient to the Lord. Because of this, I was ready when the devil came to attack my life. I had the Word of God built up in my heart and mind. I was prepared to stand and fight. It didn't matter what the doctors said or what the devil tried to make me think, my heart and mind were established in the Word of God.

When our hearts are established in the Word, we won't be afraid. Then when the enemy comes, it won't matter what he says because we know he is a liar. We don't have to be afraid of anything that comes our way because fear will leave us the moment we boldly resist the attack in the name of Jesus. As we worship God and enter into His presence, His perfect love will cast out all fear and enable us to walk in faith and victory!

## THINK BIG!
## Hang on to Hope, Faith and Vision

We need to see ourselves as champions because that's how God sees us. God has taught me to see myself His way, to have a winner's attitude and think big. I got rid of small thinking. I put hope, faith, and vision into my backpack when I climb my mountain. I can't make it to the top of the mountain with small thinking, "okay" thinking, or even "good enough" thinking. I must keep an open mind and embrace God's vision, plan, and purpose for my life.

It is God's heart to share His vision. In Habakkuk 2:2-4, the Scripture talks about writing down the vision and making it plain. I'll never give up my God-given vision. I choose to press into what God has called me to do. I align my thinking with His mind, because I have the mind of Christ.

If we want to do something for God, we have to be willing to step out in faith. We can't hold on to our own plans and ideas if we want to have all that God has for us. We can't live the great life that God has for us if we just simply try to get by. We have to increase our thinking and plan for God to step in with the miraculous. We will never see miracles if we are never in a place where we need them. We have to escape the "just getting by" attitude and dream big. We're called to overcome, not survive!

## Don't Hang on to Limitations

Shake off all limitations. Just get rid of them. Israel grieved God because they limited Him. I will try some things that may not work. Most of the things I've tried on my own have not worked.

There are a lot of different things in life that can hold us back. Being a female pastor in the South isn't easy. Many people try to brush me off because of this, but I refuse to let my gender decide whether or not I'm going to do what God has called me to do.

I could have allowed the death of my husband or the various attacks on my life to cause me to slow down. I had to choose to look beyond the circumstances, situations and problems I was facing. I had to make God's purpose for my life bigger than anything I was facing.

We all have things in our lives and in our past that we could allow to stop or limit us—the choice is ours. God is bigger than anything we will ever face. He is able to turn around and restore every broken area in our lives if we only let Him. The only one who can stop us is ourselves. We have to choose to lay aside the limitations of man and hold on with faith to the promises of God, allowing His ability to work in and through us. We may not succeed right away, but we only fail if we don't get back up and try again.

# Don't Hang on to Doubt

To reach the top of my mountain, I left doubt behind. Doubt will cause us to give up. I don't allow my problems to be the center of my attention. If I focus on doubt and keep my attention on problems and adversity, I won't make it to the top.

Problems are distractions. I must stay focused on my goal in order to reach the top. When I was on dialysis, I didn't allow that to become the center of my life. I didn't allow it to control my vision.

Let me tell you a story to demonstrate this. My late husband had a motorcycle that I hadn't ridden in a long time. I was on dialysis and was really getting weak, but I wasn't going to let that distract me. One day when I went to the clinic, I asked him to pick me up and give me a ride home on his motorcycle. He said, "What?"

I said, "Get one of those bungee cords with a hook on each end and tie me around the back of the motorcycle. Then take me home."

I was so weak from dialysis that there was no way I could sit up on a motorcycle and hold on for the whole ride home. However, I had to leave doubt behind. Doubt won't get us to the top of the mountain. Faith does not look at impossibility; faith sees victory and possibility in every situation. Faith sees that nothing is impossible with God and that we can overcome through His ability and strength.

Some people say, "Well, I'm not sure that God heals everybody." I tell them, "You have to let go of that doubt and get sure. Get to know God's will by reading His Word." The Bible says, "*... by whose stripes ye were healed*" (1 Peter 2:24). Notice here that the work of healing is already done. It says that by His stripes we *were* healed. If we *were* healed then we *are* healed.

Jesus did His part to provide our healing. Now it is up to us to receive and walk in that healing. Healing is available to whoever chooses to receive it, but we have to let go of the symptoms that seek to keep us bound. We have to look beyond them and see our miracle. We have to stand on the Scriptures and keep our confidence in God, rather than in what we feel or see.

It is not a matter of hoping we will be healed. No, the Bible says we are already healed. All we have to do is believe that we have received the promise and act like it is true. Declare what the Word says. Stop talking doubt and defeat. Start seeing yourself healed. See yourself climbing that mountain. See yourself on top of it. Then, take a step out and act on that faith.

I tell people to worship God and thank Him by faith for what is already done. The Bible says, *"Therefore I say unto you, What things soever ye desire, when ye pray, believe that ye receive them, and ye shall have them"* (Mark 11:24). We have to agree with God's Word. Never let go of it. Perseverance is the key to receiving God's results.

Some people tell me, "Well, I'm not sure that God wants to prosper everybody." I simply say, "If you doubt that prosperity is for you, then you won't prosper. You have to be sure. Read the Word. God's Word says that He has caused us to prosper. If you believe and hold on to these promises, it will remove doubt from your heart!"

I would never reach the top of my mountain if I said, "Well, I hope God's Word works. I'm not sure. You just never know. I wonder if we're on the right trail, or even the right mountain." Doubt will zap our strength. We have to stop wondering if we're going to make it and start trusting in the promises of God.

## Hang on by Passing Your Test

Before I could go to a higher grade in school, I had to prepare myself and pass the tests. No one expects to go into the next grade before they finish the previous one. It is the same with mountain climbing. We can't expect to successfully climb our mountain until we are prepared to do so. We prepare ourselves by taking the right tools, picking the right leader, and tying in to the right relationships. We have to learn to be diligent, persevere, and never quit.

The Bible tells us in 2 Timothy 2:15 to, *"study to show thyself approved unto God, a workman that needeth not to be ashamed, rightly dividing the word of truth."* Jesus told numerous parables about preparation, including the parable of the wise virgins who brought extra oil and the parable of the prudent builder who considered the cost. All of these verses talk about being prepared for what is coming up.

You can't expect to win a fight if you haven't been training. A boxer who wants to win the championship has to devote his life to training. He must hire a good coach to teach him how to box. He must watch what he eats and make sure he gets enough sleep. He must practice sparring with other boxers in order to improve. He must also study the strengths and weaknesses of his opponent so he knows his moves.

When someone is preparing to climb a major mountain, they have to do similar preparation. They train their bodies to handle extreme weather and push their muscles to get stronger. They find people who will help them in their climb. They study the mountain and learn its topography. They study weather and climate changes. They talk to others who have already climbed the mountain to find out what worked for them. They do everything they can do to prepare for anything that might come their way during the climb.

We must go through specific training during our preparation to reach the top. We need to find the right people and flow in unity with them. We have to be prepared mentally, emotionally and spiritually in order to pass our test. We will never reach the top unless we properly prepare.

## Don't Hang on to Negative Attitudes, Doubts and Fears

I can't afford to carry negative attitudes, doubts, and fears in my backpack. They are like heavy weights that will stop me from entering into God's best. God does not go against His Word. He doesn't put sickness on us. He doesn't use sickness to teach us a lesson. It isn't His will for us to be sick. That is a lie straight from the pit of hell!

When I got sick with the flu, I knew God didn't put it on me. I had opened the door to it. Sickness isn't a part of God's will. The Bible says to pray for God's will to be done on earth as it is in Heaven. There is no sickness in Heaven, so how could sickness be God's will on earth? If a person thinks that God puts sickness on them, they are deceived.

Many people, including Christians, have negative ideas about both God and themselves. Some wonder if God still loves them or if He has given up on them because of all their failures. Others think that God won't use them because they're not talented enough. Many are scared to step out in faith because they are afraid to fail.

Whatever the source of your negative thinking, it will hold you back and keep you from climbing your mountain. Holding on to fears and doubts will keep you from stepping out in faith, and if you never step out in faith, you will never see God do the miraculous in your life. You have to let go of negative attitudes in order to hold on to God and His love for you. You need to release your doubts and fears so that He can carry you wherever you need to go.

## Don't Hang on to Anger

We have to remove anger from our backpacks. Do you know how hard it is to live every day, carrying the added weight of anger? Many people go through life mad, frustrated, upset, and temperamental.

Some people say, "Well, Zona, it is just because I'm Irish that I have a temper." No, that is not it. We can't blame our anger on our race, culture or upbringing. If we have a bad temper and attitude, it's because we have adopted a bad way of thinking. God will deliver us from anger as long as we are willing to be set free. If parents have anger issues, their children will look at them and say, "Why would I want to serve God?" That's exactly what I did, because my dad had a bad temper before he got set free.

Many years ago, before my dad was set free from anger, I told him, "You scream at me all of the time. I don't want to serve who you serve. I can't do anything right. I come in late. I don't eat right. I don't drink water right. I don't think right. I don't breathe right. I can't do anything right. Why would I want to serve the God you serve?"

I was so hurt by my dad's temper that I ended up backsliding. I saw my dad take groups of young people out to witness and was upset that he seemed more concerned with ministry than he was with me. I didn't understand how he could go witness and preach all day, and then come home and yell at me. It made me not want to serve God.

Then the Lord came to my dad and said, "When Zona comes in at three or four o'clock in the morning, tell her that you love her and that I love her. She thinks that nobody loves her." That was the honest truth. Not one soul from our church came and talked to me to try to get me to come back to church. I was so mad that I hated everybody.

With many people, anger shows up when something goes wrong. Any little thing can set them off. They get upset by something as simple as running late or spilling their drink. When people have anger in their heart, anything and everything has the ability to make them mad.

After the Lord told my dad to love me the right way, he got totally set free from anger. It happened at a certain church while he was in prayer. God supernaturally touched his heart and he was able to let go of all the anger that was in him. He just felt and thought differently.

Anger is like tea in a tea bag. As long as a tea bag is sitting in hot water, the flavor of the tea will continue to come out. Likewise, the longer we allow anger to remain in our hearts, the longer that anger will manifest in our lives. We may blame this on circumstances or people, but it is really the result of the condition of our hearts and our negative thinking. There will always be situations that can make us upset, but we have to realize that we are the ones responsible for our emotions, not the circumstances.

Anger is heavy, especially if we carry it around every day. We aren't going to reach our destiny if we stay mad. If we slam the door, kick the dog, stomp around, refuse to talk, or pound our fists on the table when we get mad, we will find that is enough to make us feel like death.

If you have a spouse who acts in anger, just pray for them. We have to pray for our spouses because we married them. Keep lifting them up so that God can deal with them and remove the anger from their hearts.

We all know of people who just seem to get mad at everything. They look at life and expect the worst. They allow small things like the weather or bad traffic to ruin their day. It isn't that their circumstances are any worse than anyone else's; they just choose to respond in anger. The sad truth is that they are just mad and because of that, they won't be able to make it to the top of their mountain. Their backpack is too heavy because it is filled with anger. Learn from their example and refuse to carry anger—just let it go!

Many times people carry anger because of unforgiveness. To remove this anger from our pack, we just need to ask the Lord who we need to forgive in our lives. It doesn't matter if they were wrong and we were right, we have to keep our hearts pure before the Lord by forgiving anyone who has hurt us.

## Don't Hang on to Heaviness and Anxiety

We have to remove worry, heaviness, and anxiety from our backpacks. Jesus says, *"Come to Me, all you who labor and are heavy laden, and I will give you rest"* (Matthew 11:28 NKJV). God's peace will overtake us when we put what we can't do into His hands. If we walk around upset, angry, frustrated, anxious, and nervous, we'll find that it's a burden too heavy for us to carry. God has only called us to carry His anointing and peace.

Somebody might say, "Zona, how can I have peace?" The key is to give your problems to the Lord, rest in Him, and He will make a way. You have to live light and release the heaviness (Matthew 11:29-30). As we carry the anointing of His presence, we'll begin to walk in His rest, which is easy and light. Faith works when we cast our cares on the Lord, refusing to carry worry, fear, and pressure. Quitting is never an option! We must not allow ourselves to get so serious, frustrated, and anxious.

## Don't Hang on to Past Failures

To reach the mountaintop, I had to let go of past failures. At one point or another, everybody has been held back by past mistakes. Past failures make us say, "I don't want to try again because I tried before and messed up. I have to be careful because the last time I did something like this, it blew up in my face. I've got to watch out for myself or else I might get stepped on again."

Past failures will stop our future success by putting thoughts in our head such as, *I ended up losing everything because I went into that area. I don't want to do that again; it didn't work for me the first time.* We can learn from our past mistakes, but allowing our past failures to stop us from moving forward is foolish. To make it to our summit, we first have to let go of our past failures.

When we walk in faith, we will have opportunities to step out. We have to choose to let go of past failures so we can walk in faith, knowing that God will take care of us. We will never see the miraculous in our lives if we never step out in faith, holding on to nothing but God.

## Hang on to Obeying What God Says

The key to living in victory is found in simply obeying God's voice. I only do what God tells me to do, and you should too. That is how Jesus lived His life. He only said what He heard the Father say, and He only did what He saw the Father do. Jesus was obedient. He did nothing of His own will. So if Jesus, our example, did this, how much more do we need to obey?

We need to be like Jesus and do everything that the Father tells us to do. His commands may not always make sense to us, but God sees the bigger picture. He knows what is needed to accomplish His plan and purpose in our lives. Trust that He knows what He's doing and that He has things in place to help us fulfill our destiny.

When I was at the end of my rope, I got a grip on God's Word. It saved my life. I want to encourage you to also get a grip on God's Word, so you can climb higher than you ever have before. Cut the ties of wrong relationships and tie on to right relationships instead. Connect with people who will encourage you to reach your destiny.

I encourage you to go higher; obtain God's best and receive everything He has for you. Don't lower your standards in life. Don't settle for the average, normal, and mediocre. Hang on by getting rid of distractions and lightening your load. Live in freedom from past failures, fears, worries, struggles, and mindsets.

Let go of your excuses. Pray and confess God's Word. Obey what He tells you to do. Take a few moments throughout the day to worship God and watch as His presence overtakes you. Once you do these things, the struggle will be over. You will no longer have to live in fear, poverty, depression, failure, defeat, and oppression.

Get a grip on God's Word in order to receive God's best for your life. Hang on by staying hungry for God. Surrender your will to His. Once you do this, God's presence, fellowship, and victory will find your life. You will be able to reach this generation with God's glory, and nothing will be impossible for you. Keep your grip on God's Word and be transformed by His presence.

There is a great destiny waiting for you at the top of your mountain. The victory that God has prepared for you is so sweet. Too many Christians have settled for a life in the valley. They have accepted mediocrity and believe that is all life holds for them, but God has already provided so much more. All you have to do is climb your mountain. Determine to reach the summit and receive God's best.

You can start with this confession, saying *"Father, in the name of Jesus, I am climbing my mountain of transformation. I am going to my summit. I am fulfilling my destiny. I am unloading everything that I don't need, and I refuse to pick it up again. I am going to make it to the top and receive Your perfect will for my life."*

Now put down this book, lift your hands, and worship God. Thank Him for the victory, because the victory is *yours!*

# PRAYER OF SALVATION

God loves you—no matter who you are, no matter what your past. God loves you so much that He gave His one and only begotten Son for you. The Bible tells us that "...whoever believes in Him shall not perish but have eternal life" (John 3:16 NIV). Jesus laid down His life and rose again so that we could spend eternity with Him in heaven and experience His absolute best on earth. If you would like to receive Jesus into your life, say the following prayer out loud and mean it from your heart.

*Heavenly Father, I come to You admitting that I am a sinner. Right now, I choose to turn away from sin, and I ask You to cleanse me of all unrighteousness. I believe that Your Son, Jesus, died on the cross to take away my sins. I also believe that He rose again from the dead so that I might be forgiven of my sins and made righteous through faith in Him. I call upon the name of Jesus Christ to be the Savior and Lord of my life. Jesus, I choose to follow You and ask that You fill me with the power of the Holy Spirit. I declare that right now I am a child of God. I am free from sin and full of the righteousness of God. I am saved in Jesus' name. Amen.*

If you prayed this prayer to receive Jesus Christ as your Savior for the first time, please contact us on the Web at **www.harrisonhouse.com** to receive a free book.

Or you may write to us at

**Harrison House** • P.O. Box 35035 • Tulsa, Oklahoma 74153

# ABOUT THE AUTHOR

Zona Hayes-Morrow lives in Cleveland, Tennessee, with her husband and daughter, where she is the director of New Life Bible College, chief of staff for Norvel Hayes Ministries, and senior pastor of New Life Bible Church.

When not busy fulfilling these responsibilities, Zona is traveling and ministering where the Lord leads her. She has a tremendous testimony of how the Lord has healed her from numerous diseases, such as lupus and kidney failure.

Her burden to see God's power set people free, while meeting their needs, is shown in her everyday life as well as in her ministry.